Chairman of the Board

A Practical Guide

BRIAN LECHEM

John Wiley & Sons, Inc.

This book is printed on acid-free paper. ∞

Copyright © 2002 by John Wiley & Sons, Inc., Hoboken, New Jersey

Published simultaneously in Canada.

No part of this publication may be reproduced, stored in a retrieval system, or transmitted in any form or by any means, electronic, mechanical, photocopying, recording, scanning, or otherwise, except as permitted under Section 107 or 108 of the 1976 United States Copyright Act, without either the prior written permission of the Publisher, or authorization through payment of the appropriate per-copy fee to the Copyright Clearance Center, Inc., 222 Rosewood Drive, Danvers, MA 01923, 978-750-8400, fax 978-750-4470, or on the web at www.copyright.com. Requests to the Publisher for permission should be addressed to the Permissions Department, John Wiley & Sons, Inc., 111 River Street, Hoboken, NJ 07030, 201-748-6011, fax 201-748-6008, e-mail: permcoordinator@wiley.com.

Limit of Liability/Disclaimer of Warranty: While the publisher and author have used their best efforts in preparing this book, they make no representations or warranties with respect to the accuracy or completeness of the contents of this book and specifically disclaim any implied warranties of merchantability or fitness for a particular purpose. No warranty may be created by sales representatives or written sales materials. The advice and strategies contained herein may not be suitable for your situation. You should consult with a professional where appropriate. Neither the publisher nor author shall be liable for any loss of profit or any other commercial damages, including but not limited to special, incidental, consequential, or other damages.

For general information on our other products and services, or technical support, please contact our Customer Care Department within the United States at 800-762-2974, outside the United States at 317-572-3993 or fax 317-572-4002.

Wiley also publishes its books in a variety of electronic formats. Some content that appears in print may not be available in electronic books.

Library of Congress Cataloging-in-Publication Data:
ISBN 0-471-22889-3

10 9 8 7 6 5 4 3 2 1

To my wife, Belle, and my children Ruth, Alan, and Paul for their continued support and encouragement.

ACKNOWLEDGMENTS

Editing a newsletter on corporate governance for many years provides the opportunity to review many new and excellent books that have been written on the subject. Brief abstracts from several of these have been included in the text of this book, as it is felt that they provide additional breadth and perspective to the work. Care has been taken to provide full attribution to these authors and publishers. Frequent use has also been made of interviews conducted for *Boardroom* newsletter, as well as items of interest published in it. The thanks of the author is freely given for all quoted sources as well as to Tim Burgard and Kerstin Nasdeo of John Wiley & Sons, Inc., whose help in finalizing the manuscript and bringing this book to fruition has been invaluable.

Brian Lechem
Toronto, Canada
April 2002

ABOUT THE AUTHOR

Brian Lechem is a civil engineer by profession who, after several years in the construction industry, pursued a career as a management consultant. He has served as a director for several organizations, both in the for-profit and not-for-profit sectors, and as chief executive officer of a publicly listed Canadian company.

He was one of the founders of the Institute of Corporate Directors in Canada and was the Institute's first president from 1980 to 1982. He served as executive director of the Institute from 1983 until his retirement in 1993. During this time he acted as editor-in-chief for the Institute's publications: *Guidelines for Corporate Directors* (1987) and *The Independent Director: Recommendations and Guidance on Boardroom Practice* (1988). He has also spoken frequently at conferences and seminars on corporate governance.

In 1988 he formed Base Services Canada, a company specializing in the management of associations and organizing conferences. In 1993 he commenced publication of *Boardroom* newsletter, a bimonthly publication with a circulation approaching 3,000 available in the United States and Canada and on the Internet at *boardroomnews.com*, which focuses on reviewing and providing commentary on boardroom-related topics.

CONTENTS

INTRODUCTION

A Question of Style

There is a difference between leadership and management. Leadership is of the spirit, compounded of personality and vision; its practice is an art. Management is of the mind, more a matter of accurate calculation, of statistics, of methods, timetables and routines; its practice is a science. Managers are necessary; leaders are essential.

—Field Marshal Lord Slim,
Address to Australian Institute of Management, 1957

If there is one topic about which little has been written, and even less consensus achieved, it is the role of the chairman of the board in the North American context. The very title conjures up connotations of grandeur, like Admiral of the Fleet. In reality, the chairman of the board is probably *the* pivotal figure in projecting the image of a successful and profitable corporation.

If one were to ask the majority of board chairmen what they considered to be their primary function, one can guarantee many different responses, so vague is the concurrence. This book attempts to present an understanding of the function of chairman and to define the essential aspects of what constitutes the role. This book also will provide practical assistance to board chairmen. Much of what is included has relevance to organizations in the not-for-profit and volunteer sectors, many of which have substantial budgets and should, wherever practicable, follow closely the lines upon which a successful business is operated. Some of the key issues also have parallels. For ex-

1

ample, the vital relationship between the chairman and the chief executive officer, which is considered in some depth, has a parallel in considering the relationship between the chief elected officer, often called the chairman, and the chief staff officer of a volunteer organization, increasingly called the president.

It is also written with a view toward helping chairmen and potential chairmen of medium-size and smaller enterprises, although chairmen of large companies also may feel that this book offers practical assistance. The book will be especially useful for the first-time chairman and for the board of a recently listed public company or one soon to be seeking an initial flotation.

Even the person acting as chairman of a privately held enterprise that has outgrown the ability of its founders to handle everything themselves will find useful information in this book. The principles of sound corporate governance remain the same; only the scale changes.

ORIGIN OF THE ROLE OF CHAIRMAN

The title "chairman of the board" raises a number of interesting connotations. According to the *Oxford English Dictionary*, the word "chairman" is gender neutral, as it comes from the same root as the word "human" and is defined as the occupier of a chair of authority, the person chosen to preside over a meeting, a company, a corporate body. The terms "he," "she," "his," and "her" are frequently used within this text to reflect the fact that men and women both serve as chairmen. Perhaps Sir Adrian Cadbury puts it best in the introduction to his fine book *The Company Chairman* when he states: "I come back to the word 'chairman' because, leaving aside the seventeenth century use of the word for someone whose occupation was to wheel bath-chairs, its dictionary definition is both established and precise."[1] Wherever the term "chairman" appears, it is intended to have equal application to both sexes.

Although some people prefer to use "chairperson" or even "chair," the traditional term is more appropriate. More important, the term "chair" really confuses the person with the office. One can seat someone in the chair or, in the university sense, create a chair for a professor, but the chair denotes the office, not the person occupying it.

It is a strange thing, but the actual position of chairman is also ill-defined both from a statutory and practical aspect. Put simply, the chairman, in the context of this book, is the person whom the board

2

of directors elects to take the chair at a meeting. It need not be the same person for every meeting, and the directors in theory can choose whoever they wish from among their number to preside over their activities. In reality, they rarely do.

Legally, all directors have equal responsibilities, have one vote, and the majority prevails. Even the practice of allowing the chairman a second or casting vote is outmoded. In simple terms, if a resolution fails to receive a majority of votes, the motion is lost. Conversely, there is nothing to say that the chairman votes only if there is a tie, although some old-fashioned bylaws still perpetuate this practice. The chairman has an obligation to vote just like every other director, and in this situation an abstention is not necessarily a recommended course of action, but it does constitute a recorded vote. Further, a majority vote commits the entire board, whatever the position of individual directors, unless of course the resolution or decision is illegal or *ultra vires* (outside or beyond the authority of the board).

The development of the role of chairman has acquired increased significance in recent years. According to Cadbury:

> The pace of business activity has become more hectic and public attention focussed on companies has become greater. Companies have grown larger and more international and have extended the range of goods and services which they supply. Their growth had involved bids and mergers on an increasing scale. The public is now only too conscious of the impact which such events as takeovers, closures, and the ups and downs of trade in general can have on their lives.[2]

Because the role of chairman is evolutionary, one has to allow for a degree of customization according to the personalities involved and, importantly, the stage of development of the corporation itself. But the most important aspect must be for the chairman to ensure, as far as possible, that the board is effective and that it provides the leadership, in a strategic sense, that the company needs.

One danger is that a board may tend to micromanage: become involved in some of the minutiae of operational management that is not really part of its brief. It may consider that fulfilling its role of monitoring management is its principal focus, which it is not—it is only one of them. A chairman must maintain a careful balance between the board setting objectives for management to achieve and becoming too deeply involved in their achievement. As Cadbury puts it: "The board drives and encourages as well as checks."

One of the most frequent objections raised to boards of directors is that they still remain "old boys' clubs." In addition, membership of a board, particularly a high-profile one, is still regarded as a sinecure without specifically ensuring that the board incorporates those two key elements: competence and an appropriate balance of membership.

Therefore, the modern role of the chairman is to oversee that the board:

- Concentrates on strategic leadership and focuses on an appropriate and realistic vision
- Is constituted with a good blend of skills, experience, and business competence
- Ensures that the corporation has a realistic set of goals and objectives, and the policies, procedures, and resources in place to achieve them
- Regularly monitors the achievement of these goals and is provided with the appropriate information it needs to allow it to be effective

THE ART OF CHAIRMANSHIP

The role of the chairman is not something engraved in stone. It will vary over time according to the type and size of the organization, whether public, private, or not-for-profit, whether the organization is encountering smooth sailing or is in crisis. In fact, it will vary constantly, and the chairman's skill will relate in large part to his or her ability to cope appropriately and to motivate others to do the same.

The art of chairmanship and the ability to chair meetings are both skills that directors sometimes are asked to undertake. And yet there is currently little, if any, formal training for the position, unarguably one of the most important roles in any organization. The position of chairman of the board is complex. The person occupying it has responsibilities that include ensuring that the board fulfills its obligations and commitments, that it is organized appropriately and working effectively.

Too often, chairmen have learned by sitting on boards and from others. This informal approach does not reflect the vital importance of the role, nor does it do justice to the influence chairmen have on the quality of corporate governance exercised by the board as a whole. A good chairman must be an astute politician, a diplomat, a strategist, and a referee, and have a good head for detail. Other "hats" the chairman must wear will emerge throughout this text.

Numerous books and publications cover the field of corporate governance and are devoted to the duties and responsibilities of corporate directors. With today's increasingly litigious society and legal liability exposure for officers and directors, the need for education for directors is manifest. No longer can board members be expected to fulfill their wide-ranging and far-reaching obligations without some kind of education. Gone are the days when board positions were regarded as (relatively) well-paid sinecures without any concomitant onus to perform in a proactive manner.

One of the earliest examples of a good chairman practice that I know came when the person in question visited the offices of an organization and met with the senior executives a few days prior to the meeting, examining every item on the agenda. The staff were quizzed as to why each agenda item was required and what the objectives were. At the end of this briefing session, the chairman had decided which items were most important in terms of priorities, which items were potentially contentious, which items needed further study and discussion, and so on. As a result, the board meeting was highly productive, there were very few surprises, and contributions from all concerned were maximized.

LEADERSHIP AND STYLE

Chairmen also vary in style. Style can range from blatant autocracy to benign democracy, with a multitude of shades in between. While there is no blueprint for success, those who place themselves at the extremes will rarely achieve the best results. A small degree of autocracy may benefit the organization in times of crisis, when things are not quite as well ordered as they may be in a steady state. However, boards led by chairmen who rely almost totally on achieving bland consensus may find that some of the more difficult issues tend to get deferred. Lack of a decision can be worse than an incorrect one.

As stated, a good chairman is a prepared chairman, one who has done the homework and has anticipated problems. In most instances, several colleagues will have been sounded out and their input and support secured. In the extreme, the chairman may even suggest tabling an agenda item for further consideration rather than force a vote that

5

will divide the board rather than unite it. Consensus does not imply either unanimous agreement nor "rubber stamping." Rather it suggests intelligent compromise through constructive dialogue. The chairman's role in avoiding controversies is, therefore, very important and supports strongly the concept of adequate advance preparation.

"Instant decision making" by some board members is another cross that chairmen may have to bear. Board meetings now have to consider an agenda with very profound implications concerning risk and due diligence and the applications of appropriate levels of care and skill. The tendency to react precipitously, therefore, has to be resisted. At the same time, positive contributions from board members must be encouraged. The dividing line between remarks that show adequate consideration of an important issue and the need just to be seen (or heard) participating in an impulsive manner is sometimes very fine. The chairman must develop expert skills in guiding the board ever so diplomatically so as to achieve the desired results.

I have left the essential need for the board to apply checks and balances on the day-to-day management of the organization until the end of this introduction. Many businesses still combine the role of chairman and chief executive officer in one individual. Because of this, boards sometimes find it difficult except in the most extreme circumstances to perform their monitoring role effectively. Chapter 3 addresses the need, or otherwise, to separate these key functions. Assuming for the moment that the chairman is able to guide the board in performing the statutory need to monitor performance and, where necessary, take steps to correct an adverse situation, the chairman then must be in a position to ensure that the board is able to oversee that appropriate action is taken.

This book does not repeat in detail the basic duties of a board member, although it does provide an oversight of how the board operates and its basic responsibilities so that chairmen can become familiar with these requirements. The primary goal is to guide chairmen through the most important facets of the job and to assist them in obtaining a sound appreciation of how to perform effectively. Chapter 8 addresses the question of board effectiveness. The chairman of the board is not exempt from this assessment of professional competence. If a chairman is not performing to the level of at least a passing grade, then he or she should give serious consideration to either consciously addressing these shortcomings or passing the baton on to an appropriate successor.

There are no perfect credentials for writing a book of this nature. The experience of one individual, however broad, is invariably limited. What has been learned in one jurisdiction may not be totally applicable in another. However, besides relying on experience gained from a large variety of boardroom situations over many years, the author has consulted a number of excellent texts in preparing this book. The aim is to supplement knowledge rather than to educate from a zero base.

The issues facing boards of directors today are complex and often have profound implications both for the organization and in a personal sense. If, after reading this text, chairmen are able to consider themselves a little better prepared for the task to which they have been elected, the undertaking will have been worthwhile.

CHAPTER 1

Primus Inter Pares

The Chairman's job . . . there is no getting away from it: some sort of honour or glory attaches to the chairman's role. Almost everyone is in some way pleased and proud to be made Chairman of something. And that is three-quarters of the trouble.

—Antony Jay, author of *Management and Machiavelli*
Chairman, Video Arts, Ltd.

FIRST AMONG EQUALS

Author Geoffrey Archer is probably best known for his book *First Among Equals*, which deals with political intrigue and was later made into a television series. The prime minister of Great Britain is the subject. Some see the role of chairman as being a referee, participating little in discussion, keeping order when necessary, and making sure that the "score" is kept appropriately. Nothing is further from the truth. The chairman should be part visionary, part consensus builder, but most important a leader. In the most strategic terms, he or she should be considered the captain of the team. *Primus inter pares*—first among equals—is a good description.

The position of the chairman of the board has just a few similarities to that of the prime minister, except that the chairman's authority is not intended to be quite so all-embracing. Strictly in legal terms, the chairman is a director, just like everyone else at the board table. The chairman has no special powers. In fact, often legislation itself does not recognize the term "chairman."

Although the bylaws of some organizations grant the chairman a second or casting vote in the event of a tie, modern thinking usually dictates that the chairman casts one vote just like everyone else. If a vote does not result in a majority for the motion in question, then the motion fails to pass.

THE CHAIRMAN'S ROLE

If we cast to one side the suggestion that the chairman has some additional statutory powers, what is the basic role that he or she is expected to fulfill?

Henry S. Short, in a seminar presentation some 25 years ago to members of the UK Institute of Directors, broke down the role of the company chairman along the following lines explaining that the chairman is pivotal in ensuring an effective board as he has to perform a balancing act to be sensitive to a number of requirements at all times.

The first of these is to provide leadership style. While autocracy and consensus-oriented styles may be tolerated, in stable situations boards tend to favor a more democratically inclined manner. However, sitting on the fence and keeping score does not bode well for reaching timely and appropriate decisions.

The second is the need to structure the agenda. This should not imply imposing one's will upon the board, although with a strong personality this risk exists. It is the chairman's prerogative to maintain a balance remembering that the board's mandate concentrates more on the long-term than the short-term.

Third is the requirement to control the balance of discussion. Spontaneous "seat of the pants" participation tends to mitigate against constructive and pragmatic dialogue. Criticism should be dealt with appropriately as recrimination is rarely productive. Board members should be drawn into the discussions, yet at the same time be discouraged from over-active participation.

Actions agreed upon and decisions made at board meetings should be implemented promptly. While this is the prerogative of operational management, control mechanisms must be in place to ensure compliance. Furthermore, the agenda for the next board meeting must include reference to such action items and, if completed, there should be no need to refer to them further.

Overall, while the board's effectiveness had tended traditionally to be judged by shareholders at the annual meeting, this has little effect in the average company. It is the outside, independent, directors who should have the least to fear from being critical of a board's performance if, and this is an important condition, they are truly independent and are not concerned about tendering their resignation if the situation warrants it.

Finally, it is the chairman who usually must stand back and assess how the board is performing, and whether it is acting in the best interest of the company. It is also up to the chairman to display the courage to effect change at board level, if necessary.

Hugh Parker in *Letters to a New Chairman* covers much of the same ground but develops a checklist of six questions to be used by a chairman to test the effectiveness of the board. The term "effectiveness" is something examined in more detail later in this book, but the questions pose important issues:

1. Has the board recently or indeed ever devoted significant time and serious thought to the company's longer-term objectives, and to the strategic options open to it for achieving them? . . .

2. Has the board consciously thought about and reached formal conclusions on what is sometimes referred to as its basic "corporate philosophy," i.e., its value system, its ethical and social responsibilities, its desired image and so forth? . . .

3. Does the board periodically review the organizational structure of the company and consider how this may have to change in future? Does it review and approve all senior appointments as a matter of course?

4. Does the board routinely receive all information it needs to ensure that it is in effective control of the company and its management? Have there been any "unpleasant surprises"? . . .

5. Does the board routinely require the [chief executive officer] to present his annual plans and budgets for their review and approval? Does the board regularly review the performance of the [chief executive officer] and his immediately subordinate managers in terms of actual results achieved against agreed plans and budgets?

6. When the board is required to make major decisions on questions of future objectives, strategies, . . . etc., does it have adequate time and knowledge to make these decisions soundly—rather than finding itself overtaken by events . . . ?[1]

Thus the chairman's role is one of guiding destiny, neither preempting the board nor frustrating its participation.

In *New Directions for Directors*, author Robert Kirk Mueller explores the roles of the board itself, the chairman, and the chief executive officer.

> The criteria for the respective roles in a plural-leadership setup are elusive, organic, and tailored to suit the nature of the company, the business and the personalities involved. The elementary properties of this "fuzzy set" include the following:
>
> - Derivation and delegation of legal and judiciary power and responsibility.
> - Membership on the board of directors, and its provision for its perpetuation.
> - Emphasis on separation of board, executive and stockholder powers.
> - Reservation of certain powers for stockholders and the board.
> - Selective delegation of board powers to board committees, including assignment of leadership of committees.
> - Delegation by the board of management matters to the management.
> - Appointment of board's agent (chairman) to lead the board (this includes preparing agendas, conducting meetings, and otherwise acting as the agent of the board).
> - Appointment of the CEO [chief executive officer] to lead the management and direct the operations of the company.
> - Definition of powers reserved to the CEO, and of powers to selected corporate officers, e.g., treasurer.
> - Provisions to prevent or avoid neglect in longer-term aspects and interests of the corporation.
> - Enhancing the CEO's objectivity by providing a structure and resources which have limited political influence or competing persons.
> - Provisions for orderly succession through separation of roles and the opportunity for transition of power.
> - Provision of a check-and-balance, judicial-type process which features both the advocacy and adversary process.[2]

Three experts in their respective fields show a fair degree of correlation. It is interesting to note that Mueller is much more specific in the definition of roles and, equally important, that these be established as formal procedures. They set out a clear hierarchy: The chairman is a "servant" to the board, not its master—although of course, he or she plays an extremely important role in its operation.

WHAT THE POSITION ENTAILS

The chairman's primary task is to act as chairman of the board. Whatever other roles and responsibilities may have been allocated, that of chairing the board is his alone. One observer has even suggested that the effort made by the chairman to ensure that board meetings are properly conducted may well be the most valuable contribution he makes to the good of his company.

Many corporate commentators have suggested that numerous corporate failures in recent years had picture perfect boards, and that it was the quality of decision making that had broken down. Perhaps the Enron collapse is a case in point. The chairman is expected to exert the most powerful influence in the area of sound decision making.

One chairman of my acquaintance believed that board meetings should be conducted with all channels of communication directed through him. The dialogues and discussion tended to be one-on-one between the chairman and one of his board colleagues. The chairman's personality was so powerful that only very rarely was such dialogue extended to include other members of the board. This type of approach may be considered autocratic to an extreme.

Should the chairman feel free to express an opinion? Of course, but not in such a dogmatic manner that it tends either to stifle discussion or to fragment that important "team spirit" or collegiality that an effective board tries hard to build. The chairman sometimes may have to mediate, sometimes compromise, and sometimes adjourn debate on contentious items. But he or she should take care to maintain the board's agenda and not lose sight of the basic requirements of sound corporate governance: to ensure the long-term viability of the corporation and maintain checks and balances on operational management—in that order.

At the other end of the spectrum of chairman personalities is the "moderator," who acts with little insight and who tends to delegate much to the CEO, causing a potential conflict that is covered later. The timid chairman is discussion averse, nervous of potential conflict and contention. In other words, he or she does not subscribe to the concept of the chairman showing leadership either to peers on the board or to top management in formulating strategy and dealing with other important issues. Such an individual tends to allow discussions to meander, strong personalities to dominate, and appears to be almost oblivious to the passage of time. In case readers are somewhat incredulous, some chairmen do indeed operate at both ends of the spectrum and at many places within it.

Somewhere in between is a comfort zone that can be fairly broad to accommodate the essential personalities and chemistry that go toward the makeup of a successful board. Let us return briefly to the board meeting scenario.

I once had the educational experience of working for a chairman of a "board" in charge of a massive joint venture construction project. As project director, I was charged with managing the day-to-day operations, a kind of chief operating officer. Prior to every "board" meeting, and as it was a joint venture between several major players the membership was quite large, the chairman first used to ask us to draft a preliminary agenda of items to be discussed. Chapter 4 goes into the detail of preparing such agendas, and some of this chairman's ideas are incorporated into the text.

Next, the chairman paid a visit to discuss in meticulous detail why we wanted such items on the agenda and what our expectations were as a result of them being discussed. Did we want endorsement, approval, direction, resolution of a problem? The next stage involved the preparation of information for the board package. As a result of this briefing, we jointly agreed what relevant information would be appropriate for board members to receive to encourage the appropriate board input. This is a judgmental item but one that requires very careful consideration. Too little information renders the directors somewhat impotent to provide good decision making. Too much, or irrelevant, information similarly tends to cloud issues and hamper the most productive guidance and positive outcome.

The chairman was very careful in his preparation for the meeting. He went to great pains to brief other board members, particularly when controversial or potentially contentious issues were to be discussed. In some instances he would ask a specific director to be prepared to speak to specific agenda items, which may have involved that director undertaking additional research. In other instances, he would remove an item from the agenda that he felt required more preparation to satisfy concerns of his own, or that he had detected during his discussions with his colleagues.

Finally, at the meeting itself, he was extremely well organized, allowing discussion, even encouraging it on a free-wheeling basis, but at the same time maintaining a strict adherence to the agenda and the resolution of each item in the manner intended. His method of inviting participation was also an education. He knew, from long experience, that some directors refrained from comment when they felt they had little to add to the debate or when it was on a topic that they did not feel particularly comfortable in discussing. In such circumstances, he would be very careful not to place directors on the spot, so to speak, but would phrase a question in such a manner that they felt comfortable in responding constructively.

LEADERSHIP

So far two specific aspects of the position have been discussed, chairing board meetings and relationships with top management. We now have to consider that other important function: leadership. A chairman must initiate and inspire policy. A chairman must develop a sense of vision and a clear idea of where the company should be going. In many companies today this process, if undertaken formally, tends to be called strategic or long-range planning (see Chapter 5). This is not quite what is intended in this context, although such a process is extremely important.

A chairman of a very large public company with almost 30,000 employees worldwide once told me that part of his role was to be able to detach himself from the day-to-day routine and just dream. His free-ranging thought process sometimes extended from the sublime to the ridiculous, but it allowed him to venture outside the boundaries of the company's more immediate objectives and relate to the character and philosophy of the businesses that they were in and those in which there might be some benefit in becoming involved.

Traditionally the chairman now acts as spokesperson for the company. To fulfill this role, the chairman must be well briefed and have the required temperament, personality, and public speaking skills.

The need to act as the public focus comes with the territory. It is not something that should be delegated lightly to a top executive manager, even the CEO, or to someone responsible for publicity or public affairs, although these people could undertake some functions jointly. According to circumstances therefore, the chairman, if neither a natural nor a trained speaker, must acquire the necessary abilities. The chairman also must ensure that various crisis, and even disaster, scenarios are considered and rehearsed and that briefings are prepared ahead of time to allow him or her to react appropriately.

Most companies, even some of the very largest, are ill-prepared for a major predicament. The media has a voracious appetite for certain types of news, particularly news that is classified as potentially sensational. A wrong or inappropriate reaction may cause a company incalculable harm. Imagine, for example, if Johnson & Johnson had not dealt with the Tylenol tampering crisis in a correct manner. The classic case of *Smith v. Van Gorkum*, which precipitated the legal liability crisis of the mid-1980s, resulted from a company improperly responding to a takeover bid. In times of crisis, the chairman also may need to meet representatives of financial institutions and major investors—not to discuss specifics necessarily, but to maintain public confidence in the corporation.

If the chairman has financial, public relations, and even legal responsibilities, it follows that he or she must be provided with the necessary staff support. Where the chairman is nonexecutive, as against being an employee, the line authority to provide such services may rest with the chief executive officer. However, such a pivotal individual as the corporate secretary, for example, must relate closely to the chairman and both advise and fulfill many of the support functions that will enable the chairman to be the most effective.

Cadbury states "The authority to get things done—to execute—is not dependent on having executive responsibility for people."[3]

Chapter 11 goes into additional detail on the important topic of dealing with the outside world.

CHAPTER 2

Building the Board

We have to evaluate almost everything that happens in industrial and commercial organizations. Yet there is one area about which little is generally known, let alone measured, which by common consent is the most important of all—the way in which a board of directors works.

—Brian P. Smith, Managing Director,
PA Management Consultants, 1972

This chapter talks about building a team. It discusses chemistry and synergy and it tries to place in perspective the characteristics required of North American directors who are, for most parts outside, independent, and, in the words of the Toronto Stock Exchange Guidelines, unrelated to management. Ideally, such directors also should be independent of majority shareholders; with the concentration of ownership particularly prevalent in North America, this is not always achieved.

Independence in the context of representing the interests of *all* shareholders equally and without bias is sometimes an oxymoron. If a major shareholder has the right to nominate a director to a board, is it expected of that director to promote the interests of that shareholder to the extent that other, perhaps minority, shareholders may potentially suffer, be ignored, or, in the extreme, be oppressed? Unfortunately, however desirable it is to act strictly in accordance with the law (which does not distinguish between any class of shareholder), human nature, and perhaps the concern for retaining the appointment or pleasing the nominator may cloud the exercise of true unbiased judgment.

This is why, in representing the interests of all shareholders equitably, it is so important to realize the team concept at the board table, where consensus building is paramount. It is also where preparedness to compromise is a regular consideration, provided the quality of decision making does not suffer, and where dissent is reserved for the ever so rare occasion when it becomes really necessary.

Having said all this, the chairman's role in helping to assemble the eclectic board is of paramount importance. Assembling does not imply the unfettered right to choose one's board colleagues, nor does it mean a regime of autocracy that can undermine individual character and personality in arriving at unanimity. Rather it means molding a team of diverse skills and expertise into an effective top decision-making body, despite potentially conflicting pressures and interests.

THE SELECTION PROCESS

In the longer term we are all agreed that no business—whatever its product superiority, its financial resources, or excellence of its management and workers—can run without proper direction. To quote from *The Independent Director* by William Houston and Nigel Lewis: "Independent directors are only as good as the chairman will allow them to be. It is fruitless for a competent person to join a badly run board—that is unless they have the proxy vote for a large block of shares. It says little for an individual's reputation and judgment if he or she accepts a directorship only to discover the board's work is paralysed and he has to resign."[1]

Unfortunately, the director selection process often is badly flawed. In theory, shareholders elect directors at the annual general meeting. In private and closely held companies, theory may be followed to the extent that the annual meeting elects the directors, but in reality the owners choose them and the rest is a formality.

Even in widely held companies, shareholder participation is rarely sought. The "old boy's club" still operates quite effectively in some circles, and most nominations are made by the chairman, the CEO, or other senior existing members of the board. Increasingly, larger companies form nominating committees that operate with a degree of independence, but a recent survey in *Boardroom* newsletter (Jan/Feb, 2001) confirms that personal acquaintance is a disproportionately important factor in the director selection process. True, outside advisors

17

such as legal counsel, auditors, and executive search consultants do sometimes help, but this occurs in a minority of instances. Also, the advisors often search for a specific area or type of expertise, or, unfortunately, to obtain token representation or to take account of geographical interests. In defense of these practices, exponents truly believe that selecting someone already known to stand for election is likely to be a more successful process than bringing in an outsider.

But why appoint outside, independent, directors? There are many reasons, some of which will be gone into in greater depth later. Among these reasons are objectivity, detachment, the ability to stand back and discern the "forest from the trees," and bringing additional experience or expertise (in the broader sense) to the board. Perhaps most important, they provide an essential forum, independent of operational management, to maintain checks and balances on the corporation and to decide policy and future strategy.

In setting the scene for the selection of outside directors, the pitfalls and concerns regarding their appointment must be noted. While serving as an outside director previously was considered by many to be a sinecure, even an honor, today accepting directorship of a board now can be anything but a straightforward decision, for two reasons.

1. The time commitment is considerable, in terms of both attendance at board and committee meetings, and essential reading to satisfy the fairly demanding due diligence requirements imposed by the courts to avoid the potential for undue litigation.
2. In the current litigious climate and legal liability exposure for directors, almost every potential director is now making extensive inquiries to protect their net worth as far as prudently possible before accepting board appointments.

To quote from *Non-Executive Directors* by Kenneth Lindon-Travers:

A characteristic of searching for a non-executive [director] is that it invariably brings not one but two potential benefits to the hunter. Finding the right body is an obvious one. The second, in importance a surprisingly close runner, is the quite revealing insights into the role which results from meeting with people who have expressed enough interest in the appointment to join in exploratory talks. . . . The sequence leading to the appointment . . . should be demand led and not supply driven; in fact, the reverse is frequently the norm. Searchers who take the easiest route generally favour amiability and blandness, favouring people who are already known quantities, or prefer to maintain only a vague image of the target in the hope of meeting with an available candidate whose credentials can become an agreed specification."[2]

By replacing the words "bland" and "amiable" with "compatible chemistry" and "common philosophy," we might improve the quality of director selection. Even better, is it not now appropriate to pass the baton for board selection to a properly constituted nominating committee? By so doing, some of the problems of self-perpetuation, lack of objectivity, and lack of policing management would not occur. While personal recommendations still should be placed before the committee, several other component parts to the selection process should be considered as well.

One of these is to draw up a single-page requirement, or job specification. This listing will set out the specific requirements of the position (quite separate from the desirable characteristics). Items to be included in this brief are:

- Makeup of the current board, their roles and primary strengths
- Specific supportive input required from the director being sought
- Likely requirements in terms of committee membership and special assignments
- Schedule of meetings and approximate total time requirements, including reading board papers and minutes, travel
- Specific features in terms of personality, style, age, and chemistry
- Target appointment date
- Any other special factors

ACHIEVING A BALANCE

How does one set about building an eclectic board? Let us assume that there are no appointments preordained by major shareholders and that one can start with a clean slate. Then consider some of the less desirable types of appointments, not because the individuals concerned may be unsuitable but because of potential conflicts of interest or heavily skewed professional backgrounds. J. M. Wainberg, QC, in the text of *Duties and Responsibilities of Directors in Canada*, was quite clear in asserting that lawyers should not combine the duties of providing legal advice with sitting on the board.[3] Not only was this a potential conflict, but in a possible legal action, the lawyer/director has been, and could well be in the future, held to a higher standard than his or her colleagues.

Accountants who act in a professional auditing capacity are precluded by their professional body from sitting on boards. Similarly, bankers and others who provide professional services should not be placed in a position of providing a service (for which they or their employer may receive remuneration) and sitting as an independent director.

At the other extreme, many boards try to recruit outside directors who hold, or have very recently held, senior-line management responsibilities—CEOs of nonconflicting companies, for example. Unfortunately, however enticing such appointments may be, there are rarely enough people so qualified to fill all the available board vacancies.

In between is a vast potential inventory of qualified individuals who would make very good independent directors and benefit the companies on whose boards they may be invited to sit. Ideally one should seek a blend of expertise that complements the activities of the enterprise. Someone with senior-level retail experience may not necessarily be a good fit for a heavy-machine manufacturer. According to Lindon-Travers:

> Co-directors expect their non-executive [i.e., independent] directors to have a number of specific personal qualities in addition to experience and skill. Each prospective non-executive should measure his or her capacity to be:
>
> - An effective and persuasive communicator whose contribution is concise, objective and clear.
> - Socially competent with a touch of humour.
> - Independent of mind without prejudicing loyalty to colleagues and the board.
> - A good listener who can focus on key issues and respond with sound advice.
> - Democratic in balancing the interests of shareholders against the interests of others involved with the business.
> - An achiever in his or her particular chosen field.
> - Constructive in expressing ideas and opinions, even when critical.
> - Able to perform effectively as an individual when divorced from the structure and props of his or her own organization.
> - Unimpressed by either the prestigious or the financial aspects of the appointment.

- Positive in making statements and proposals, and unwilling to acquiesce in silence.[4]

The chairman needs to ensure that the nominating committee brings sufficient objectivity to the process of both searching for new director talent and, over the course of time, renewing it. Such a committee, on which the chairman may wish to sit or chair (although independence from the chair may be an advantage) should consist of not less than three and certainly not more than five senior independent members of the board, depending on its size. Average board sizes now range between 10 and 12 members but can be smaller for more modest-size companies and larger for major enterprises. However, the trend is definitely toward the lower end of the spectrum commensurate with sufficient resources available for equitable committee obligations.

Many boards attempt to obtain some balance by specifying different disciplines or expertise and experience that should be brought to the boardroom table. In some circumstances, particularly with highly visible public companies, other quotas come into play: women, geographical representation, ethnic minorities, native groups, and so on. Competence as a director is now of such importance to the governance of the corporation that it should *never* be compromised. While, all things being equal, board representation should be appointed to represent specific interests, in real life, all things are rarely equal, so sometimes a fine degree of judgment must be exercised.

Lindon-Travers discusses "forced choice appointments," or nominees selected by particular shareholders, investors, or other interested parties who have the specific power to nominate directors. According to Lindon-Travers, about one in every five appointments to United Kingdom boards is as a result of nominee arrangements. This situation raises a much more serious problem, unfortunately honored more in the breach: representation of all shareholder interests equally, a statutory requirement. However, often directors represent certain shareholdings and apply selective pressure on the board. Would we be faced with so many cries to represent minority shareholder rights if all shareholders were invariably treated equally? But this opens a much wider spectrum of corporate governance debate.

If nomination rights are afforded to special interests, all the board can do is try to use moral and ethical persuasion to ensure that they perform their roles appropriately and that their nominees bear in mind all of the philosophical and strategic balances that a board should strive to achieve.

CREDENTIALS AND QUALIFICATIONS

The individual qualities Lindon-Travers considers necessary for independent directors tend to relate to personality rather than experience. Many other authors have drawn up their own lists of desirable characteristics. Brian Smith, former managing director of PA Management Consultants, provides one of the most succinct lists of criteria considered fundamental for a board appointment:

- Breadth of business experience and outlook, preferably at board level, in successful organizations.
- Capacity for long-term thinking and planning and an ability to analyze quickly.
- Financial sense and a working familiarity with accounts and reporting systems.
- Ability to communicate in a straightforward way.
- Limited number of other significant directorships.
- Similar approach to business.
- A particular functional background, but not if it unbalances the board. A current executive job helps to keep feet on the ground.
- Not least, independence, both financial and intellectual, is essential so that views can be expressed under no constraints whatsoever.[5]

The *Handbook for Corporate Directors,* edited by Edward P. Mattar and Michael Ball, adds a few additional abilities:

- Sufficient financial and cost-accounting expertise to serve on the audit committee, work with outside auditors, judge the adequacy of corporate financial controls, and understand all of the company's finances.
- Ability to judge people and their personnel qualitatively and quantitatively.
- Sufficient familiarity with securities laws to ensure compliance with a securities commission, stock exchange requirements, federal and provincial rules and regulations.
- Ability to contribute to the formation of corporate policies, plans, and objectives.
- Recognition of what must be supplied by management so the directors can carry out their duties properly.[6]

What this list illustrates is that the qualifications for appointment as an outside independent director are quite substantial and onerous. If a potential director has most of these attributes, chances are that he or she will be able to perform extremely competently.

The term "business experience" does not necessarily mean experience in the same type of business or even in the same industry sector. Any related experience can be useful. The link becomes tenuous only when there is so radical a distinction between types of business that other attributes become more pronounced, such as similarity of business philosophy. However, experience as a successful businessperson should be considered an essential prerequisite, as practical exposure to decision making is many times more valuable than theoretical knowledge or acting purely in a support role. Being in business essentially involves risk. Not every business decision results in a positive outcome, and those who have experienced adversity and emerged successfully from such situations are far better placed to react to the unexpected than those who have not.

It is almost axiomatic that outside directors should have a similar approach to business philosophy as their colleagues on the board. Otherwise their differences could lead to contention and unnecessary divergence of views, which ultimately can prove time-consuming and counterproductive.

Business experience is not the same as financial acumen. One of the greatest sources of business failure is a profound lack of understanding of the potential financial consequences of decisions and actions. Since one of the board's major responsibilities is to monitor the ongoing operations of the enterprise, board members must have a high degree of familiarity with reporting systems and the ability to discern and interpret potential risk. The intuition to perceive impending problems is another strength.

Independence—financial, intellectual, and in its broadest sense political—is essential so that views can be expressed without constraint. An outside director, unless a substantial shareholder in his or her own right, has only two major weapons: the power of persuasion and the ability to resign. If the director relies on the board appointment as a significant source of income or is beholden for some other reason, he or she may not speak out strongly in opposition to something that should rightly be opposed. Such a person will find it much simpler and easier to go along with the forces of power and may demonstrate a feeble objection by abstaining from voting on important matters.

Independence really comes into its own in crisis situations, but it also has a bearing on the whole conduct of board meetings. Some board chairmen, particularly those who combine the role with that of chief executive, may find it difficult to acknowledge that at board meetings they are first among equals. What may be excellent traits in an operational sense—aggressiveness, forthrightness, tenacity, determination, courage of convictions—may have less of a place in the arena of collective responsibility. Often the outside directors are left to apply checks and balances to prevent overzealousness that could lead ultimately to disaster.

At the other extreme, some chairmen always insist on rule by consensus. If this approach fails to achieve unanimity, a chairman may succumb to inaction or adjournment of major decisions. This is not a satisfactory conclusion either. The outside, independent, directors must have sufficient clout to insist that appropriate action should be taken, particularly when time is of the essence.

The late Sir Kenneth Cork, an eminent chartered accountant who specialized in bankruptcies, wrote in his foreword to *The Code of Practice for the Non-Executive Director:*

> For many years it has been the practice of public companies to have on their boards non-executive [outside] directors. Originally, they tended to be persons who, by their name or reputation, gave credibility to the company from the public's point of view. Often, these directors did not feel that they had a duty to see that the company was properly run, and that they should exert influence when it was appropriate. This resulted in many jokes about "guinea pig" directors.
>
> In my professional experience, I have come across many companies which have fallen into difficult times, only to find that their nonexecutive directors were conspicuous by their absence from the problems of the company. . . . I hope that this Code of Practice indicates the standard which is required of these persons:
>
> (a) They are people to whom the auditors can talk, either through the audit committee or off the record, about the problems they find in investigating the company's affairs.
> (b) They are people who should assess impartially the ability of management and, if appropriate, even take the necessary action to remove both the chairman and the chief executive officer.
> (c) They are the people who should be prepared to stand up and be counted.
>
> Those who take on the job of being a non-executive [outside] director will, I am sure, increase the standing and accomplishments of

the companies they join—if they fail in their duties then their "licence" to be non-executive directors should be withdrawn.[7]

REMUNERATION OF INDEPENDENT DIRECTORS

What should an outside director be paid? Lindon-Travers says: "Enough, but not enough to matter, is the golden rule. When an outside director is there for the money, independence is in jeopardy."[8]

Until comparatively recently, directors in Canada in particular generally were paid much too little, but according to a survey published in *Boardroom* newsletter, recently this amount has increased substantially.[9] The average aggregate remuneration, according to the survey, was around Can$28,000, made up generally of a retainer of around Can$19,000 and Can$1,000 per meeting attended (including committees) with half this amount paid for attendance or involvement by electronic means or by the use of teleconferences. Some sectors, for example financial, invariably pay at the high end while manufacturing and some high-technology companies pay below average. However, the grant of stock options should be taken into account in determining remuneration.

Recently stock has been used as part of the compensation package. Again, according to the survey, nearly three-quarters of companies now pay at least part of the remuneration package either in stock or the grant of options. Some companies go further by insisting that directors acquire a meaningful stake in the company as part of their commitment to the enterprise. As one director put it when asked to invest US$100,000 as the "price" of his board seat: "There is nothing that concentrates the mind as much as an investment which ranks alongside one's mortgage."

Comparative U.S. dollar packages can be for upwards of 50 percent more. In the United States, directors are paid significant amounts that reflect, among other things, the premium of the U.S. dollar over the Canadian. However, there are other significant differences as well. In Canada, the average director attends six or seven board meetings a year and probably devotes about the same amount of time to briefings and consideration of board minutes. In the United States, an average board appointment is expected to consume about 20 days a year *plus* committee time, which could add another 10 days a year per committee, plus "homework." Thus, in the United States, directors are expected to devote at least 30 days to their position, approaching double the average Canadian allocation of about eighteen days (but with large variations).

In deciding on an equitable level of remuneration, the first consideration is commitment. A director should be remunerated sufficiently to take his or her appointment seriously, to attend board meetings, and to devote sufficient time to board responsibilities so as to demonstrate complete competence in the role. The era of token directors is past. A company has a right to expect, and directors must be prepared to give, sufficient time to do justice to the requirements of the position.

The second consideration reflects the legal liability exposure and ensures that directors perform diligently and to the depth necessary to protect shareholders' interests—and their own. Some of the decisions required of directors today are extremely onerous, particularly in the fields of disclosure, mergers and acquisition activity, and in regard to environmental matters. The board must be proactive. Remuneration must reflect this type of business climate.

A third consideration must relate to the quality of corporate governance. Shareholders—and this includes the increasing influence of institutional investors—demand performance. Today, performance reflects varying amounts of risk. The quality of decision making at the board level must demonstrate this. In precisely the same way in which management is remunerated with packages that take into account the value added to share prices, directors must, at least to some comparable degree, be compensated appropriately.

But as Lindon-Travers says, remuneration must not be enough to matter. The integrity and independence of outside directors must not be affected. This is a difficult balance to achieve, but responsible attempts must be made. Survey comparisons are useful but should be considered guidelines only. The modern approach to compensating directors tends to follow more along the lines of a systematic job evaluation assessing degree of involvement, responsibility, commitment, and competence, as outlined earlier.

Apart from reimbursement of expenses and such precautions as providing legal liability insurance coverage, directors should rarely receive payments beyond those already mentioned. In fact, any optional perquisites or inducements should be considered very carefully if there is any likelihood that the director's independence will be jeopardized. Intellectual and financial independence are two principal

26

mainstays of an outside director appointment. Compromise either of them, and the integrity of the whole board is at stake.

It is useful to discuss the terms of an outside director's appointment while discussing remuneration. Invariably, corporation bylaws require directors to be re-elected either annually or after a maximum three-year term. It would be useful for the board to consider prescribing maximum terms of office, say 7 to 10 years, after which an outside director has to retire to allow the infusion of new blood. It has become increasingly common for directors to undergo regular performance evaluations; those who receive a failing grade with no subsequent improvement may be eligible for automatic retirement. While this situation may seem cold-blooded, these are tough, highly competitive times. Boards have not performed well in too many instances; directors should be informed up front what is expected of them, rather than be embarrassed by nonperformance at a later stage.

How much should a board chairman be paid? Here the figures vary widely depending on whether the appointment is considered essentially part time *and* nonexecutive in character or whether a significant amount of time, such as a couple of days a week on average, is required. If the former, between Can$5,000 and Can$15,000 can be added to the director's remuneration package. If the latter, a very wide range of figures are used, from about Can$60,000 to over Can$250,000. Obviously the size of the organization plays an important role in deciding the appropriate package. A good guide for an executive chairman role would be to assume a per-diem rate around the average fees paid to professional advisors.

ORIENTATION AND TRAINING

There appears to be a growing acceptance by boards that directors, particularly those newly appointed, should have some induction and orientation to the company on whose board they now sit *and* some training in the role and responsibilities accorded to independent directors, particularly of listed companies. For some reason, surveys consistently indicate that approximately 50 percent of boards and directors, in general, fail to pursue some rational director training program. Indeed, as far back as 1995, in making a presentation to the Canadian Senate Committee on Banking, Trade, and Commerce, respected outside director Sir Graham Day stated that:

New board members badly need a directors 101 training course. A first time parent and a first appointment to a public company are two very responsible roles for which, in our culture, we demand little if any preparation. . . . [A training program] would cover topics such as relevant legislation and the fundamentals of corporate law, stock exchange regulations, good corporate governance practices, basics of strategic planning, organizational behaviour and personnel matters.[10]

I spent many years in the volunteer sector, involved with the Boy Scout movement as a group-level leader before eventually becoming a commissioner. The movement is particularly active and successful worldwide in organizing comprehensive and continuing training for its leaders of all ranks. At one training course, a wizened and obviously charismatic scout leader questioned why people like him needed training. The answer given to him was that some leaders are born, some leaders become leaders by being trained, but all leaders become better leaders with training.

The same has to apply to directors. Some directors seem to have the gift of adapting to the role almost intuitively. But, in reality, there are very few such people. After they overcome the exhilaration that sometimes comes with a board appointment, most directors learn by sitting quietly and observing. Bill Dimma, an experienced high-profile independent director, relates one of his very early board appointments:

... The chairman put down the paper from which he had been intoning, removed his glasses carefully, and looking down the long table at me, said solemnly: "Welcome, Mr. Dimma, to your first board meeting. I'm sure you'll find it a most interesting board. There is only one thing I wish to say to you. It is and, for many years, has been our custom that a new director is not expected to speak during his first year of board service." I nodded blankly.[11]

Induction and orientation are quite different from director training. Many companies take the trouble to provide newly appointed directors with a briefing kit containing past board minutes for, say, the previous six months to a year, the current and previous financial statements, organization charts, any specific and key decisions recently taken or ongoing, and so on. The briefing kit could well include information about the company's mission and vision, its current strategic plan and the current year's budgets, and, most important, something about the philosophy of the organization, although many directors will have sought that information before accepting the position.

Next the orientation might include introductions to the other board members, senior members of staff, visits to all locations where the company operates, and an in-depth briefing about the current and planned activities in which the company is engaged. This element of the introduction is mechanistic and often is assembled in a manual that includes communications, company policies as they may affect the director such as expenses, and any other background material that will enable the newcomer to be brought up to speed.

Training involves specific techniques. The role and responsibilities of the director is one key area. Legal liability exposure is another. Most directors could truly benefit by embarking on the entire educational program outlined by Sir Graham Day.

Regrettably, the need for promoting director competence is not something that has yet appealed to many directors, although we can only hope that in time it will. As an editorial in *Boardroom* states:

> The dearth of competent director talent may not be overwhelmingly apparent at the highest corporate echelons, although undoubtedly there are some companies that could benefit from a director educational "tune-up." The major problem exists in the medium-sized and smaller listed public companies where boards cannot attract the more experienced talent. In these circumstances, director education and training is an invaluable resource. This is all the more essential in the light of the emphasis being placed on the management of corporate risk—that multi-headed monster that most boards only appreciate on a microscopic, as against a macroscopic, basis.[12]

IF THINGS GO WRONG

A whole section of the Institute of Corporate Directors' booklet *The Independent Corporate Director* deals with anticipating boardroom problems.[13] Readers who wish to go into more detail on this subject should acquire this publication. I have already mentioned the problem of legal liability exposure. Outside professional advice is one means of minimizing this exposure. Another method is to insist on full documentation and prior warning of major decisions. Still another is to make sure that the company has procedures in place to ensure that statutes and regulations are complied with, that financial records are complete and accurate.

However, situations can exist where there is, for example, less than fully competent management; inadequate or untimely information systems; lack of planning or operating systems and procedures; misguided loyalties; or even lack of respect for the board and reluctance to submit to its authority. Any or all of these situations can make for a very uncomfortable scenario where a director may conclude that he or she is being placed at risk and may not wish to continue as a member of the board.

Obviously, the first thing the director should do is discuss the problem with the chairman of the board and, if necessary, with other outside directors. The important thing is to ensure that such matters are being considered objectively and not from an emotional perspective. Sometimes sensitivities run high for ridiculous reasons. Very few people take kindly to criticism, even when delivered in the most tactful and constructive manner. Possibly the best thing to do should a confrontation occur during a board meeting is to adjourn the meeting to allow passions to cool. One chairman insisted that contentious matters never be discussed at board meetings, preferring to ventilate them in private sessions, one on one, or in small groups, until an acceptable compromise was achieved.

But sometimes the pressures of the situation demand more urgent action. Most important of these could be when a director feels that the board is either exceeding its authority (acting ultra vires) or behaving unethically or, in the extreme, illegally. In these situations only a few options remain, and these are covered more fully in other publications. Resignation may remove the director from the immediate scene of conflict, but residual legal liabilities may remain. In such circumstances, the need to seek competent professional advice cannot be emphasized too strongly.

In one situation, a director resigned from a board and almost two and a half years later the company went into liquidation. You can imagine his surprise when he found himself sued, in common with all other directors, both present and past, by a major bank, for many tens of millions of dollars. The bank claimed that it relied on actions taken (or not taken) by the board during the director's tenure many years previously. Eventually the action against this director was discontinued, but not until many thousands of dollars had been spent in legal fees.

Being an outside director probably never has been a sinecure. Today it is probably just as difficult to find suitable directors who will agree to an outside board appointment as it is for someone to agree to accept one. But the whole basis of free enterprise depends on sound corporate governance. Somehow or other, balance must be achieved.

CHAPTER 3

Separation of Roles or Concentration of Power?

Unlimited power is apt to corrupt the minds of those who possess it.

—William Pitt, Earl of Chatham
House of Lords, January 1770

ONE JOB—OR TWO?

James Gillies, in his book *Boardroom Renaissance*, is quite outspoken on the subject of the interrelationship of the chairman and the chief executive officer.

> The balance between the CEO and the board is a delicate one. Usually, the CEO, particularly if he is also the chairman, is very much in charge. He controls the agenda, the flow of information to the board, has massive knowledge of the affairs of the company, makes recommendations of senior appointments, handles capital spending initiatives, . . . so the board sees the corporation very much through his eyes.

Gillies goes on to state that

Clearly the CEO holds a great deal of power, in fact if not in law. This power is further enhanced because board members normally have considerable respect for expertise and are not inclined to challenge a CEO before his peers unless the issue is very important. . . . Peer pressure is great and oftentimes is limited and so, the CEO, if he is also the chairman, controls the meeting.[1]

And here is the crux of the problem as stated by J. W. Lorsch and E. MacIver in *Pawns or Potentates: The Reality of America's Corporate Boards*: "[Thus a situation exists where] there is a power reversal between CEOs and directors. A situation in which directors are supposed to govern a more powerful CEO, who in most cases is also chairman of the board, is rife with complexity and ambiguity."[2] Most authors on this subject, including Gillies, accept that there is, and should be in well-managed enterprises, always "some creative tension among the board, controlling shareholders (if there are any) and the senior executives. Such tension does not imply lack of confidence or trust of one for the other, but is a reflection of the different responsibilities of each. When such tension is lacking it usually means that someone is not meeting his obligations."[3]

In an interview with Dean Roger Martin of the Rotman School of Management at the University of Toronto, Martin was asked how a board can maintain an appropriate oversight on a strong-minded CEO:

This is a tough challenge. Why is it daunting—it is simply the information asymmetry. Management will always have way more information than the board will. No amount of board briefing will overcome this. The CEO has lots of information, the board some. . . . If the CEO wants to obscure information such as "how hard will it be to accomplish budget goals?" it could be well-nigh impossible for the board to discern. However, if there wasn't this information asymmetry, and the board knew as much as the CEO, then it should fire him![4]

So a board must maintain checks and balances on management. If the most senior employee manager is the chairman of the board as well as CEO, the task is not only intimidating but difficult because the CEO can control the flow of information and control the agenda.

Nevertheless, many organizations do combine the roles of chairman and CEO, despite exhortations to the contrary by practically every major authority, including the recently published Saucier Report (see Chapter 7). How do boards in which the roles are combined fulfill their checks and balances responsibilities?

Before suggesting one or two methods, it would be appropriate to discuss the separate functions of the CEO and the chairman. The first point to note is that they are two quite separate jobs. The chairman serves as a strategist and leader, as well as consensus and team builder. The chief executive officer is expected to be a leader also, but, in addition, a strong tactician, a good people manager with a head for detail, someone who is outstandingly flexible in outlook and results oriented.

According to Robert Mueller:

> The establishment works in normally predictable ways. The historical career movement is for senior executives to go onto the board, and then one of them becomes chairman in a classical succession flourish. However, this pattern does not recognize the difference in requirements for being a good chief executive officer as distinct from being a proper director or chairman of the board.

Mueller also talks about the "Siamese Twin Syndrome":

> For a company where the chief executive is acting also as the board's agent, i.e., the chairman of the board, we have a "Siamese twin situation." It is hard to separate the reactions and inter-relationships of the executive from the director or steward function. This coupled situation provides for increased vulnerability. Further, it does not recognize the legal and social significance of keeping the board of directors as a separate part of the institution dedicated to provide checks and balance.
>
> Where this Siamese twin syndrome exists is a good place to watch for problems in the future. While a competent, capable person performing these two roles can often take hold of a company in serious trouble and lead it out of the wilderness, in the long run it should be a matter of concern to a proper director to keep these two roles separate.[5]

INTERRELATIONSHIP OF THE ROLES

The main point is that the role of chairman essentially is different from that of chief executive. Human nature being what it is, not everyone who makes a good CEO is able to translate successfully into the role of chairman. I was once approached by a man who had run a company very effectively for many years until it was acquired by a much larger international corporation. The man was asked to become chairman of what was now a major subsidiary and, at the same time, was invited to take a seat on the parent company board.

His new bosses made it quite clear that they did not expect him to have any part in day-to-day operations, so initially he was at loose ends. Fortunately, he was able to see the totally different character of the chairman's role. Although there was some internal struggle, it was expected that, over time, his vast expertise and industry knowledge would be invaluable in the strategic and oversight role that was now demanded of him.

Notwithstanding the need to assume new and different responsibilities, the chairman was acutely aware of the need to create a close working relationship and understanding with the CEO who had assumed his original responsibilities. The ability to act as mentor was relatively easy. What was much more difficult was to come to terms with the fact that now in charge of operations was someone else who may have different ideas, different methods, and different people-handling skills for achieving the results and objectives demanded of him.

Keeping hands off operations is one thing. Becoming a board chairman and concentrating on a new set of imperatives is another. Perhaps it is now more apparent why combining the two roles into one person may be fraught with difficulties, not the least being the ability of the remainder of the board to control the chairman/CEO.

There have been many high-profile corporate situations in recent years where it has been found necessary to change the CEO. In many instances the change occurred well after it had become apparent that something radical needed to be done. Many of these circumstances involved a CEO who also held the position of board chairman. By virtue of personality, character, and often sheer forcefulness, the CEO/chairman could intimidate boardroom colleagues to the extent that they deferred action longer than was necessary.

By virtue of the power of the two positions, the CEO/chairman can maintain control even when a company is failing. In some instances, control has been retained by means of selective presentation of information. In others, the chairman/CEO provided plausible explanations, and the directors were hesitant to challenge them. In yet other situations, it became evident in retrospect that the board had been deliberately misled—perhaps not necessarily in a criminal sense, although rarely this may have happened, but misled to the extent that the true situation was concealed.

When the roles of chairman and CEO are combined, boards must be especially vigilant in maintaining the diligent oversight demanded of them.

BALANCING THE ROLES

The Cadbury Committee Report produced for the London (UK) Stock Exchange entitled *The Financial Aspects of Corporate Governance* includes a section called "The Code of Best Practice" for the board of directors. The following abstracts from the code explain one method of addressing the combined role of chairman and CEO:

Item 2   There should be a clearly accepted division between the head of a company which ensures a balance of power and authority, such that no one individual has unfettered powers of decision. Where the chairman is also the chief executive, it is essential that there should be a strong and independent element on the board, with a recognized senior member.

Item 3   The board should include non-executive [independent] directors of sufficient calibre and number to carry significant weight in the board's decisions.

Item 4   The board should have a formal schedule of matters specifically reserved to it for decision to ensure that the direction and control of the company is firmly in its hands.[6]

Obviously the Cadbury Committee was well aware of the risks in combining the role of chairman and CEO, and its members imposed clear initiatives as to how the situation should be dealt with. Indeed, the *Combined Code* now adopted by the London Stock Exchange for all publicly listed companies has made it a requirement to separate the functions or provide valid reasons for noncompliance:

There should be a clearly accepted division at the head of the company between the chairman and managing director. The justification is to try and ensure a balance of power and authority, such that no one individual has unfettered powers of decision. A decision to combine the posts of chairman and managing director in one person should be publicly explained.[7]

In implementing the recommendations of the Dey Committee in 1994, the Toronto Stock Exchange had a slightly different approach.

It proposed 14 guidelines that were not intended to have a statutory effect. However, all publicly listed companies had a statutory obligation to report compliance or otherwise in their annual report or information/proxy circulars. The relevant guideline covering the topic of chairman/CEO relationship (now reinforced and, to a degree superseded, by the report of the Saucier Committee) is rather long:

Guideline 12　　Every board of directors should have in place appropriate structures and procedures to ensure that the board can function independently of management. An appropriate structure would be to:

1. Appoint a chair of the board who is not a member of management with responsibility to ensure the board discharges its responsibilities, or,
2. Adopt alternative means such as assigning this responsibility to a committee of the board or to a director, sometimes referred to as the "lead director." Appropriate procedures may involve the board meeting on a regular basis without management present or may involve expressly assigning the responsibility for administering the board's relationship to management to a committee of the board.[8]

Either of these methods might work. Whether it is a desirable compromise is another matter. Clearly the trend is moving fairly rapidly toward separating the chairmanship from the executive role.

However, the vast majority of large North American bank structures do combine the roles of chairman and chief executive. To quote from an interview with Blair MacAulay, the lead independent director at the Bank of Montreal:

We have had a lot of soul searching on this subject. [It] would seem that banking is a special case. In North America the head of the bank is regarded as being the chairman, not the CEO. We have in place a number of checks and balances to pre-empt abuse of power. In our bank, the lead director chairs a session at every board meeting without inside directors present, where board members can make their views known without inhibition. We measure the performance of the chairman and CEO very stringently, both as chairman of the board and a director, and separately, as CEO.

The important thing is that there must be mechanisms to relieve pressure. These have to include communication links so that concerns may be brought up. If these do not exist, and there have been some publicized instances in recent history, then pressure builds until the board is forced to get rid of the chairman/CEO occupying the combined role.[9]

THE CHAIRMAN'S JOB IS DIFFERENT

Many books define the chairman's job and how it is so very different from that of the head of operations, the chief executive officer. According to Sir Adrian Cadbury the responsibilities of chairmen to their boards are to ensure:

- that the board provides leadership and vision;
- that the board has the right balance of membership;
- that the board sets the aims, strategy and policies of the company;
- that the board monitors the achievement of those aims;
- that the board reviews the resources of the people in the company;
- that the board has the information it needs for it to be effective.[10]

However, while this list is of vital importance, it leaves out much of the detail necessary for the first-time chairman to be able to understand *how* to perform. Besides, while it is impressive to be able to state "that the board provides leadership and vision," there must be a catalyst at work to mold the board, and that catalyst is the chairman of the board. But let there be no doubt about it: The chairman is the agent of the board and acts as its servant. Her authority is, or should be, clearly defined by the board to act on its behalf and not in her own right.

In some organizations there is an executive chairman (i.e., a full-time or substantially full-time employee of the company) rather than a nonexecutive chairman. While it is common in the United Kingdom and some other countries within the British Commonwealth for the chairman to be essentially an employee of the company and to be paid a salary to reflect this time commitment, the practice is not yet widespread in North America—although it is growing. This situation reflects the increasing complexity of governance and the important distinctions between operational management and corporate direction, which have been much more clearly defined.

To assist in defining the role and responsibilities of chairmen, it is useful to define what turns out to be a substantial set of tasks. One of the better descriptions is set out by David Leighton and Donald Thain in *Making Boards Work*: "It is the chairman who has the most influence on how effectively the board operates and whether it works as what we term 'an old-style' board (perfunctory, superficial, and impotent) or as a 'new style' board (vigorous, creative, and empowered). The chairman, therefore, has a major influence on the relationship that develops between the board and the CEO."[11]

Exhibit 3.1, from Leighton and Thain, presents a possible job description. As it is all-embracing, not every role described will be applicable in every circumstance.

Since Leighton and Thain's text was published in 1997, much attention has been devoted to the topic of risk. This quotation from Kevin Brown serves as a useful postscript to the exhibit: "[The board]

Exhibit 3.1   Chairman of the Board—Outline of Job Description.

1	**Managing the Board**
(a)	Chairing meetings of the board
(b)	Setting meeting schedules
(c)	Setting meeting agendas
(d)	Managing directors' performance
(e)	Communicating with directors between meetings
(f)	Controlling meeting attendance
(g)	Determining board information packages
(h)	Helping appoint committees
(i)	Determining director compensation
2	**Developing a More Effective Board**
(a)	Determining board contribution
(b)	Planning board composition and its succession
(c)	Ensuring the recruitment of new directors and the "retirement" of those who are ineffective
3	**Working with Management**
(a)	Monitoring and influencing strategic management
(b)	Building relationships

Exhibit 3.1 (*Continued*)

(c)	Helping define problems
(d)	Monitoring and evaluating performance of the CEO and senior officers
(e)	Representing shareholders and the board to management
(f)	Representing management to the board and to shareholders
(g)	Maintaining accountability by management
(h)	Ensuring succession plans in place at senior management level
4	**Managing Shareholder Relations**
(a)	Chairing annual and special meetings of shareholders
(b)	Meeting with major shareholder groups
(c)	Accompanied by the CEO, meeting with financial analysts
(d)	Accompanied by the CEO, meeting with financial press and potential sources of debt and equity capital
(e)	Communicating with shareholders and potential shareholders
5	**Liaison with Other Parties**
(a)	In conjunction with CEO, representing company to public, suppliers, customers and staff
(b)	In conjunction with CEO, developing relationships and representing the company with governments, regulators and government agencies
(c)	As requested by CEO, working with competitors on industry problems
(d)	Liaison with CEO and management
(e)	Representation on other boards
(f)	Public service and leadership role, with the CEO, in charities, educational and cultural activities

Source: David S. R. Leighton and Donald H. Thain, *Making Boards Work: What Directors Must Do to Make Canadian Boards Effective* (McGraw-Hill Ryerson Ltd., 1997), p. 147. Used with permission.

must reach consensus about the significant risks to strategic objectives and make sure that clear decisions have been made about how risks are monitored and who is to do it. There needs to be clarity about the design, implementation and responsibility for the review and monitoring process."[12]

IT IS LONELY BEING A CHIEF EXECUTIVE

The role of the CEO can be very isolated. All CEOs desperately need to know how they are performing. This need to obtain an independent opinion is not at all a sign of weakness. It is recognition that no one is perfect and that there are many ways to "skin a cat." In addition, because they are strongly orientated toward operations, CEOs sometimes may benefit from the opinions of those who are able to stand back and see the forest and not the trees.

CEOs can gain this broader perspective in two ways: (1) by consulting with peers, the management team; and (2) through board involvement.

Peer consultation should take place as a matter of course in any democratically run company. Yet the problem of autocracy can arise, as does the inescapable thought that the CEO is ultimately the boss and has the final word. The problem in involving one's peers is the natural fear of criticism. Subordinates are usually reluctant to criticize a superior, particularly in front of others, and it needs a very well adjusted superior to accept such criticism, even if proffered in the most constructive manner.

Through board participation, CEOs can discuss concerns on a higher and more dispassionate plane. While a highly desirable practice, companies that lack this capability to act as a sounding board tend to experience difficulties more readily than those which do not.

This fact leads to the monitoring role of the board. Increasingly companies are introducing some formal performance evaluation mechanisms. Traditionally, many companies have used the performance appraisal approach as a tool to develop, motivate, and reward. It brings a necessary degree of objectivity into what has sometimes been a subjective, even an emotional, environment.

Chief executive officers therefore need to know their specific goals and objectives both as head of operations and also as director. Committees charged with assessing the objectivity of the appraisal system within a company and ensuring, as far as possible, common standards, know that sometimes people obtain superior performance in adverse circumstances. It is important to judge and discriminate whether achievements have been made by the CEOs themselves, or whether they have occurred due to circumstances largely beyond their control. As it has been said, anyone can make a fortune in a bull market. It takes a genius to make one when it's in free fall.

In an address to the Institute for International Research Corporate Governance Congress, Thomas Kierans said the following in regard to publicly listed financial companies:

> [I]t is not just a question of market performance of the stock on a year over year basis. In economist's jargon, there are exogenous factors as well as endogenous factors to be considered. Exogenous means simply that if you are CEO of an interest rate sensitive company and interest rates go down, then you are going to do pretty well regardless and didn't have a single thing to do with it![13]

In companies in which the CEO is chairman of the board as well, a strong independent presence is essential as initially promoted by Cadbury, but much more strongly by the more recent Saucier Report. Where the roles are separate, the chairman of the board must spearhead strong interaction with the CEO to ensure the fullest support and encouragement. According to Kierans: "The relationship [of the board] with the CEO has to be carefully managed. . . . When a new CEO is appointed there should be scope for mentoring by the chairman and other senior members of the board. But everything must be so structured so that the CEO is in charge of managing the company, and nothing must be done to detract from this vital responsibility."[14]

SUCCESSION PLANNING

One of the most important roles of the board is to safeguard CEO succession. However, most companies wait far too long before considering both the current situation and the process of renewal. Historically, when considering the fortunes of a typical company in the two to three years prior to when a change of CEO becomes necessary, one would often find that overall corporate performance has been flat, or is even declining. It is comparatively rare for CEOs to leave on a high note.

Therefore, the first thing a board should do in evaluating CEO performance is to detect a period of relative mediocrity as early as possible rather than be complacent and wait until the situation demands more urgent action. The more lead time available, the smoother a future transition is likely to be. This does not necessarily mean an expression of CEO dissatisfaction, which could demotivate the individual or even cause a premature departure. It can mean a time for the introduction of fresh blood, new ideas, a change of direction, all of which can be presented in a positive light. By far the best CEO transitions are achieved with the support of the current CEO.

Another challenge often facing boards is whether insiders should be groomed for the succession role or an outsider recruited. In the latter case, substantial additional expense and learning curve are involved. Historically, it has been found that insider successors often perform equally well as outsiders. If the process is handled carefully, an insider promotion can only benefit the company. The problem often lies in the fact that prudent organizations tend to nurture two or even three potential CEO successors. When the appointment is ultimately made, the losing finalists, key employees usually with a wealth of valuable experience, often depart in short order. The effect of their departure depends on the strength of the company's remaining top managerial talent.

If CEO succession is managed well, the positive results frequently appear quite soon after the appointment is finalized. Managed poorly, the company suffers rapidly, and it takes time to recover the situation. The key is somehow to persuade the current CEO to be an integral part of the succession process. If the CEO is approaching normal retirement, the process is easier. Once board members become aware that corporate growth and achievement of strategic objectives are leveling out, one of the warning signals, CEO contingency planning should begin. The chairman, if different from the CEO, or the lead director or chairman of the nominating committee if not, has a primary role to play in the process.

The planning of succession must be rigorous and objective. It must include an evaluation of the competencies and skills required of the CEO. Comparative external data should be obtained wherever possible, either by industry or by similar size and type of enterprise. The board should also establish its succession objectives and the time within which these should be achieved. In other words, the process should have a definite sense of purpose. If appropriate, consideration should be given to establishing a separate board working party, a "selection committee," explicitly to manage the strategy and its implementation.

As part of the customary process of evaluating senior management, the board generally insists that the CEO regularly assesses the performance of all senior colleagues and lists how their abilities can be developed further. This process is, perhaps, a subtle way of encouraging the CEO to groom one or more potential successors, if need be by expanding their experience and expertise within the enterprise. If CEOs are reluctant to embark on this kind of subordinate development process, the board has an obligation to bring pressure to bear so that they do so. Again, this is not necessarily an easy task but should be achievable.

The board must be aware that there are a number of negatives to consider. The current CEO may be status conscious and fear loss of face and earnings, or even be reluctant to consider leaving the company. Therefore, constructive steps must be taken to allay such concerns by replacing them with positive aspects, such as pension or performance bonuses, stock options, and the like. There may be opportunities for the current CEO to be nominated to serve on other corporate boards. The board should carefully consider creating an incentive to make a change, and do it sooner rather than later.

The ad hoc selection committee should prepare the specifications for the CEO's job carefully. The specifications should both be incisive and realistic, containing all the perspectives necessary, including outside references as appropriate. Of course, the selection process must be conducted under conditions of strictest confidentiality. No director, even when checking references or insider information about potential candidates, should do so unless specifically charged, and at the appropriate time. Premature disclosure often causes morale problems and may even deter potential candidates.

The benefits of choosing an insider are continuity, a built-in support network within the company, and less risk. It also sends a positive message to others within the corporation regarding the potential for advancement. Choosing an outsider allows the company to change direction more easily. The process can bring fresh ideas, and there is far less temptation to stick with tradition. An outsider CEO can, for a listed company, send a positive message to the stock exchange, particularly if the stock price has fallen below that of its peers.

There are definite risks associated with the CEO succession process. At worst, the newcomer can fail to perform as hoped, and it becomes necessary to start the whole routine over again. It is important to treat insider candidates in precisely the same dispassionate manner as outsider candidates. Otherwise comparison of attributes becomes difficult. Selection committees must resist the urge to place weighting on the talents and qualifications of candidates interviewed earlier. It is important to consider everyone on an equal footing, including pursuing references diligently. Finally, in negotiating the remuneration and benefit packages, an equitable balance must be struck between existing policies and those that apply to the new CEO. Nothing destroys morale quicker than perceived inequity. Most boards try to achieve an appropriate balance between reward and future potential by the judicious use both of short- and longer-term incentives based predominantly on personal achievement of well-specified objectives.

CHAPTER 4

Establishing the Agenda

Business more than any other occupation is a continual dealing with the future: It is a continual calculation, an instinctive exercise in foresight.

—Henry R. Luce,
Quotes for Everyday Inspiration,
CCH Canadian

One of the most important roles of the chairman is to organize, structure, and chair effective board meetings. Without a clear focus, board meetings can become unproductive, meandering, frustrating, lack purpose, have a tendency to overlook or disregard warning signs—in fact, not fulfill even the basic concepts for which they exist.

The principal purpose of holding board meetings is to make sound decisions. These decisions can range from routine to those that may have a profound impact on the company's future. A meeting will generate the best results only when all the participants are fully briefed and contribute to the highest practicable levels of sound judgment and decision making.

THE BOARD IN ACTION

Before discussing the board meeting and its agenda, a number of other topics should be addressed. The operation of all incorporated corporations are covered by legislation, either federal or at a lower level, such as state or provincial. This legislation governs legal requirements and imposes many challenges in respect to the effective operation of the board. How decisions are made is a vital component of this. The principle of collective responsibility and the distinction between direction and management must be defined so that directors understand them. This chapter provides some of the key practical elements regarding how the board should function. It covers the planning and holding of board meetings and the selection of the agenda and explains some of the more important shortcomings of boards of directors.

The purpose of board meetings is to deal with an agenda. In other words, the meeting must be planned and not left to informal, unstructured discussion. Traditionally, the "board" has been viewed as the locus of power. The board is seen as the focus for all those key decisions on which the future of the corporation rests. The 1994 report of the Toronto Stock Exchange Committee was entitled *Where Were the Directors?* In no cases should the board, under the chairman's leadership, be accused of either abdicating or shirking its responsibilities.

To whom is the board responsible? Modern practice lists several interested stakeholders, beginning with shareholders and including the company, suppliers, creditors, employees, and society as a whole. However, since shareholders elect the directors and the directors occupy a position of fiduciary responsibility to safeguard the assets of the corporation on behalf of shareholders, clearly the board's actions should give high priority to shareholder interests.

Yet the board also has a primary duty to the corporation, since directors act as agents of the corporation. Therefore, which has priority, the company or the shareholders? While the answer to this question is sometimes complex, in simple terms directors act both as agents and as trustees. They owe duties to the corporation, their shareholders, their fellow directors, creditors, employees, and the public. As agents, they are charged with the responsibility of managing the assets to gain profits. As trustees, they are charged with the responsibility for preserving the assets, but they are not the owners of these assets. In most situations, these interests ultimately will coincide. Comparatively rarely will a board have to make a value judgment preferring one party over another. However, court decisions have made it clear that should a conflict arise, the body corporate usually should be considered first.

Before getting too far into the actual mechanics of board meetings, it is essential to define some important constraints imposed on directors.

THE PRINCIPLE OF COLLECTIVE RESPONSIBILITY

There is a fundamental difference between a senior manager and his interaction with subordinates, and the chairman of the board and his interaction with his board of directors. To quote an extract from an excellent little handbook, *Guidelines for Directors*, published by the Institute of Directors:

> Although the wise senior manager will always attempt to carry his subordinates with him, possibly using the device of a management committee, both he and they know that the manager has the ultimate power to issue instructions [expecting them to be obeyed]. He manages *in* committee, not *by* committee.
>
> Although a chairman of the board may occasionally say "sometimes we count the votes and sometimes we weigh them," the same principle does not apply to a board's deliberations. A board seeking to achieve a common view about an uncertain future should reach decisions by which all its members agree to be bound. It therefore manages *by*, not *in*, committee.[1]

It follows that although board decisions may be taken formally and the voting recorded, neither the chairman, nor any other member of the board, has authority to impose his or her will upon others. Even though the democratic process is adhered to, it is fundamental to the operation of a board of directors that all members are bound by consensus.

What the principle of collective responsibility means in every day terms is much more powerful. Even if a director either votes against or abstains from a motion, he or she is bound by the decision of the majority and, by law, is equally liable together with the other members of the board for the implications of such decision.

The principle of collective responsibility obviously has its shortcomings. What happens, for example, if a director feels that something inappropriate or, in the extreme, illegal is being undertaken? There are various procedures available to a dissenting director that can range from simple resignation (and this eventuality is dealt with later in this book) to putting one's objections in writing to the company and to the appropriate government department. These are extreme actions and, in the overwhelming majority of circumstances, disputes are almost always resolved by dialogue.

Obviously, for the principle of collective responsibility to work and the board to act as a cohesive and harmonious body, consensus must be reached most of the time. Some of the techniques available to achieve this will be referenced later. However, if the board members are not bound by a common business philosophy or have a reasonably high degree of personal chemistry, this does not bode too well for the future. Perhaps this is why a good chairman of the board is sometimes hard to find.

Another definition that is important in understanding the role of the board is the distinction between direction and management.

DIRECTION AND MANAGEMENT

Direction and management are basically in conflict. A shareholder who is also a director has to distinguish between the roles of shareholder and of director. A director who is also a full-time executive of a corporation must distinguish between the roles of director and manager. It is perhaps too simplistic to suggest that a director's role is strategic whereas a manager controls tactics, or that a board makes strategic decisions while management implements them. The distinction may become a little clearer if one states that directors normally need not, indeed should not, be concerned with the day-to-day operations of the corporation.

But what about the full-time executive, or manager, who is also a director? The most obvious example of this is the chief executive officer. If the CEO is the sole inside representative, what is called the "two-hat" concept—where a senior member of management has to balance that role with that of a director—is unlikely to be of concern. On the other hand, if the chief operating officer is also on the board and, perhaps, the chief financial officer and/or an executive vice president, there is the potential for additional conflict.

Management has the responsibility to implement and directors have the responsibility to maintain oversight (i.e., checks and balances on management). Board members may find it necessary to take a position that reflects criticism of a member of management who is also a director. It is possible that, at the board level, a manager who is also a director can be placed in a position of criticizing a management colleague to whom he may be subordinate in an operational sense.

A scenario involving this predicament occurred with the board of the National Ballet of Canada in the late 1990s. It is important to remember quite clearly the role of the board and the responsibilities of directors. If these duties are discharged responsibly at the strategic level, it should be possible, in most instances, to avoid personal situations being drawn into the decision-making process.

A board composed of too many inside directors as against outside or independent ones may encourage the development of "yes men." The director's role, almost by definition, is to challenge. However, how likely is a subordinate to question the actions of the boss at a board meeting? Herein lies a major challenge.

HOW THE BOARD WORKS

According to William Houston and Nigel Lewis in *The Independent Director*:

> One fundamental difference between a board and a management meeting is the presence of independent directors who are not responsible to the chief executive. They are there to form a critical mass which should ensure that the executives responsible for tactical control of a business are obliged to take into account the strategic long-term future and to weigh the sometimes conflicting interests of the various parties. . . . The board is run by the chairman who is responsible for [the] board agenda, conduct of meetings and the preparation of correct minutes. He also has the responsibility for representing the company to the outside world.
>
> The board formulates corporate aims that are acceptable to a spread of shareholders who may not have common objectives. Some may be long-term investors who do not mind whether dividend payouts are subordinated to creating long-term cash flow; others may be short-term investors who wish to maximise their return.

The board ensures that it has a sound future strategy and [that a] plan is established to manage the business in line with these aims. It also watches out for early warning of changing business conditions or competitive pressures that may require changes to the plan. It ensures that the company has resources, particularly money and people, sufficient and capable of implementing the strategy.

The board ensures that financial systems are accurate, timely, will deter possible fraud and represent assets at their correct value. It monitors performance against the plan and takes corrective action if necessary. [Finally], as well as its prime obligation to the company and trusteeship for shareholders, the board fulfils its obligations towards employees, customers, suppliers and the community.[2]

STATUTORY RESPONSIBILITIES

Due to the extent of current legislation, directors are exposed to an extremely wide range of legal liabilities. It is useful to understand the overall scope of these liabilities.

First, the legislation under which businesses are incorporated states that a director must be loyal and act honestly to "exercise the degree of care, diligence, and skill that a reasonably prudent person would exercise in comparable circumstances." Under common law prior to these acts or bills, directors did not need to exhibit in the performance of their duties any greater degree of skill than might reasonably be expected from a person of their knowledge and experience. It is probably correct to say that the acts usually restate the common law standard in modern terms, reflecting the fact that the overall level of competence and skill of directors has increased significantly. Compliance with the acts is still essentially subjective in nature. There is probably not a "reasonably prudent director" test under this definition.

Recent legislation and the courts' interpretations of the law have become much more stringent. A degree of proactivity is now almost always required. Accordingly, directors must almost invariably show they have applied due diligence before they can defend an action against them successfully.

Furthermore, directors are assumed to be jointly and severally liable for actions taken by the board. This is the principle of collective responsibility coming home to roost. Directors can seek some comfort in obtaining director's and officer's liability insurance against wrongful acts, but there still remains a strong onus upon them to know the basic concepts of the law as it affects them and to obtain more specialized professional advice when necessary. It is worthwhile remembering that directors are at risk to the extent of their total net worth. No one would wish to be at risk of losing this hard-earned wealth if it can possibly, and prudently, be avoided.

Essentially, directors' liabilities arise from a number of areas, including:

- *Liabilities arising from legal duties.* These liabilities arise from the legislation previously mentioned.
- *Liabilities resulting from equitable responsibilities.* Directors and officers of a corporation have fiduciary duties vis-à-vis the corporation. They are not allowed to enter into situations where they have, or could have, personal interests conflicting with that greater interest of the corporation they are bound to protect.
- *Liabilities regarding purchase of shares, dividends, and borrowing.* There are well-defined liabilities with regard to these and other actions taken by the board. The acts specify these liabilities in more detail.
- *Liability of directors for wages, severance payments, withholding taxes, and the like.* The legislation sets out very strict rules regarding the above, and recent labor reform laws have made the position even more challenging. Generally speaking, directors must ensure that monies belonging to others—for example, the government—are paid promptly and that funds remain available to discharge liabilities to employees.
- *Liabilities regarding winding up, insolvency, bankruptcy, and so on.* These liabilities are specialized areas where directors may be liable. Professional help is always strongly recommended.
- *Liabilities under environmental protection legislation.* This is a relatively new area where directors may be exposed to substantial penalties. It may be advisable to obtain reference materials in this area. For example, *Environmental Protection Legislation*, published by the Institute of Corporate Directors, explains the fundamental situation in Canada in simple terms.

The board also has certain statutory responsibilities, such as preparing annual accounts by certain deadline dates and circulating them to shareholders, filing the accounts, tax and other statutory returns, holding annual shareholder meetings, and so on. Once again, these matters are extensive and are outside the scope of this book.

BOARD PROCEDURES

The more formal procedures relating to board operation should be set out in the board manual.

> The board manual can provide a guide to help directors of a corporation to do their job. Since no two corporations are completely alike, no two board manuals will be identical. A manual that does not reflect the character, the culture, the needs, the stage of growth, and indeed the aspirations of its corporation will not serve its board well.
>
> The board manual is not a formal legal document. It should not be confused with a charter, constitution or bylaws. Its principal value is to guide and facilitate the board in discharging its duties. . . . Nearly everyone agrees that the board is responsible for top management succession, perpetuation of board membership, long-term corporate objectives and directions, and such key functions as support, guidance, review, advice, and approval of management decisions. With or without a board manual, directors would evolve a process of responding to management.[3]

Boards operate so much better with a clear understanding of all these key areas. It is difficult to understand how so many boards function without this kind of definition of board procedures. In precisely the same manner that a CEO draws up a job description for a newly appointed manager, the board also must draw up its own roles and define which directors or committees fulfill these functions. The description can set out mandates for each of these functions and define limits of jurisdiction and responsibility. It can even establish a program of routines to ensure nothing gets left to chance or omitted.

Three major areas of board responsibility must be considered on a regular basis.

1. Compliance reviews
2. Items concerned with the company's ongoing operations
3. Decisions that the board should make

Compliance reviews embrace statutory requirements, such as government-stipulated returns, withholding taxes, and the like, and compliance with regulatory matters such as competition, health and safety, environmental matters, labor codes, antidiscrimination, and so on. Under this heading also falls discussion and approval of annual and quarterly financial statements (for listed companies) and appropriate and timely corporate disclosure documents. Also included are such items as major contractual obligations (e.g., covenants contained in loan agreements, dividend restrictions, collective labor agreements). These reviews also should cover the corporation's social conduct—labor relations, environmental protection, community and government relations, and so on.

Items relating to the ongoing operation of the business must be dealt with systematically. Care must be taken to resist the temptation to spend too much time on history. Nothing can be done about events that have already happened. Excessive time is often spent on postmortems rather than focusing on the future, either to take corrective action where necessary or to plan future strategy.

The board must come into its own in the area of decision making. Here the board cannot shirk or delegate responsibility. Examples range from simple approval of financial statements; agreeing arrangements for new banking facilities, to approving a new prospectus for a stock issue, dealing with a takeover bid, and so on.

CHOOSING THE ISSUES

Inevitably the board agenda must be structured to cover the full spectrum of responsibilities. However, many boards tend to spend too much time reviewing the past rather than looking forward. We shall assume that regulatory matters are being dealt with. The corporate secretary and legal counsel are the best people to guide the board in this respect, and their advice should not be taken lightly. This discussion assumes that *all* reports have been circulated to the board ahead of time and, apart from clarification or approving actions that should already have been taken to correct adverse trends, there will be little further discussion on this historical aspect of the agenda.

What should the board consider as major issues to be addressed? Obviously, any major contingency that has arisen and that cannot, or perhaps should not, be dealt with by management alone must be raised at this juncture. Examination of major corporate failures invariably demonstrate that the board has been slow to react, if at all, to impending signs of major problems in these cases. When action was taken, usually at CEO level, it was usually too little, too late. Therefore, the consideration of risk is an extremely important matter to be considered.

The only way to avoid the chance of a major omission from the board agenda is to cover systematically, in the course of a year, every major topic with which the board should deal. Examples of these topics include:

- Financial results
- Year-end decisions
- Annual general meeting
- Manufacturing
- Marketing
- Financial policies
- Strategic plan review
- Annual budget approval

None of these topics should be dealt with without adequate preparation. Management must prepare and circulate comprehensive position papers well ahead of time and be prepared to discuss these papers with individual board members prior to the scheduled board meeting. If major recommendations are embraced in any of these position papers, they must be presented formally with justification and backup provided. Finally, time must be allowed, if necessary, for outside independent professional advice. This time may be necessary either to satisfy the need for the directors to demonstrate due diligence in the legal sense; and/or to verify independently or to expand on some of management's proposals.

INFORMATION FLOW

The questions invariably asked in regard to briefing directors prior to a board meeting are: How much information should directors be provided, and how much should they be entitled to ask for?

Briefly, directors should be provided with everything they ask for, and they are entitled to ask for any information they like. However, in legal terms, directors demonstrating due diligence are not expected to go behind, or into, the books or information provided but must make sufficient inquiry to satisfy themselves that the information is, on balance, both accurate and realistically presented. After all, directors must have some trust in management. Without this, the whole framework of the corporation, and the trust embodied within it, will collapse. There are many ways of presenting information and the established format must be clear, concise, and accurate.

At least one and preferably two weeks prior to each board meeting directors should receive enough financial information concerning operations to enable them to judge corporate performance. They also should receive a complete agenda listing all matters that they must consider, including supporting material. Where appropriate, this supporting material should include all committee reports.

All committees without exception report to the board. A committee is formed at the board's pleasure, and no committee decision ever releases any director from accountability for its actions. Such important committees as the executive committee (if one exists), the audit committee, the compliance review committee (for financial institutions), and the human resources and compensation committee all are accountable to the board. The minutes of all committee meetings should be available to all directors, although, in certain circumstances, appropriate confidences should be respected.

The corporate secretary plays an important role in keeping directors informed of relevant news releases and other disclosures, quarterly filings and reports, publications prepared for both internal and external distribution, the annual report, proxy circulars, and statutory filings. This flow of information will keep directors informed fully of the corporation's activities and helps them in making informed judgments about current decisions and future strategies. Being informed will enable directors to avoid "shooting from the hip" or "seat-of-the-pants" participation. Unprepared directors—those who either have not had the time or the inclination to brief themselves properly—tend to use these techniques to demonstrate involvement. Proper information flow also ensures that the directors have the opportunity to ask questions, seek clarification, or even discuss among themselves prior to the board meeting items that may be sensitive, potentially controversial, or crucial to the future of the company.

THE REAL AGENDA IN DECISION MAKING

The key to all successful meetings is the agenda. The best chairmen go to extraordinary lengths to ensure that the agenda chosen is the most appropriate in the circumstances. Furthermore, any sensitive or contentious issues must be dealt with in such a manner that consensus can be reached.

In one case, a chairman prided himself on never bringing controversial matters to a vote, preferring to remove items from the agenda or defer final consideration until a small working party or subcommittee could address the matter outside the board meeting. Then directors were approached, sometimes individually, for their views. The chairman tried to seek a universally acceptable outcome or an appropriate compromise. In this manner, while the chairman avoided confrontation, the decision-making process often was prolonged unnecessarily.

Unfortunately, the exigencies of real life do not always offer us the luxury of tabling an item for a future meeting. Sometimes difficult problems must be addressed head-on without delay. This is not to say that consultation between directors cannot take place prior to the meeting, nor does it mean that a short adjournment cannot be called to allow a heated atmosphere to cool. But at times most boards will have to address contentious or controversial issues; they must be prepared for decision making in such cases.

Board minutes serve as vital records of proceedings. For the statutory minute book, the corporate secretary, or whoever is taking minutes, should record all decisions at a minimum. He or she also should record key items in the debate leading up to such decisions without necessarily (unless considered important) making attribution to a particular person. However, should decisions not be unanimous, it is important to record negative votes and abstentions if requested.

Sometimes a second set of more complete minutes is produced to facilitate the implementation of decisions made. These minutes sometimes are referred to as management minutes; explanations are provided regarding the rationale the board used in arriving at its decision. These more detailed minutes usually do not pertain to sensitive or confidential matters so that they may be circulated to senior members of management who will be charged with acting on the results of the board meeting. They are usually distributed at the discretion of both the chairman and the chief executive officer.

Minutes should always be recorded in sequence, as they occur, and be numbered in a unique manner. Sometimes the numbering system reflects the date of the meeting, but this is optional. Where action must be taken as a result of a board decision, this should also be reflected in the minutes as well. Conventionally, the minutes should be signed by the secretary upon dispatch and countersigned by the chairman upon approval at the next board meeting. Convention also sometimes dictates that the minutes be passed in front of the chairman before circulating them to other board members. However, this is more of a courtesy rather than a statutory requirement. The person who records the proceedings is responsible for preparing the minutes; he or she must resist the temptation to "doctor" or massage them to reflect something different from that which took place.

BOARDS THAT DO NOT DIRECT

By definition, directors should ask questions. Questioning is an essential element in the process of due diligence, so board members can satisfy themselves that the conduct of the corporation's affairs remains satisfactory. Traditional (and perhaps outmoded) thinking, however, is that directors should not ask too many questions, and should not ask embarrassing ones that might appear critical of the chairman, CEO, or management. "Troublesome" directors find that their terms of office may be short-lived, and their "reputation" could spread so that they do not receive invitations to sit on other boards. How far directors should question and how much they should reserve for outside the meeting is a judgment call. However, directors should never feel intimidated about asking questions on matters of importance.

Directors who are major shareholders or nominees of one have more secure positions. High-profile outside directors also can be major interrogators with relative impunity. After all, who wants the embarrassment of a well-publicized resignation? Directors must be objective questioners for their own good, for that of their colleagues, and to contain their legal liability exposure.

The era of rubber-stamping must end. Directors must be proactive. They should not agree to matters that are insufficiently explained or justified. Remember, it is the directors' job to direct and management's job to manage. The two functions are totally different.

However, there is still ample room for tact and diplomacy. In most instances, board meetings do not have to be confrontational. If directors do their homework and seek clarification or additional information prior to board meetings, many potential problems can be sidestepped or resolved. Board members also must discuss sensitive situations with each other outside board meetings. Clearly, the chairman should play a pivotal role in all of this. But what happens if the chairman also is CEO? Holding dual positions could complicate the situation.

The power of a chairman who also holds the CEO's job is disproportionate. Modern thinking, as already stated, strongly supports a separation of the roles. However, should directors feel that the two positions could potentially conflict, the outside, independent directors must get together separately without any members of management being present to discuss the situation and decide how to deal with it, preferably outside the boardroom.

The buzz words "proactivity" and "acting diligently" remain. In this current litigious climate, there is no way that directors can allow themselves, and the board as a whole, to react passively to the workings of the corporation. Directors must never allow themselves to get out of touch. Nor must they allow themselves to be convinced without sufficient searching inquiry. Ignorance is no excuse, since it is the director's job to keep informed. If the company does not provide sufficient information, it should be requested. The key, however, is exercising judgment as to how much to ask for and what questions to ask.

CHAPTER 5

Setting the Direction

Surround yourself with the best people you can find, delegate authority, and don't interfere!

—President Ronald Reagan, 1984

Chapter 9 devotes some attention to strategic principles in reminding directors, and chairmen in particular, that the board should focus on the future and not become embroiled in operational management. The principal errors committed by boards, particularly in smaller and medium-size companies, is to concentrate on extremes—either attempt to micromanage or maintain too much of a hands-off profile without maintaining necessary checks and balances.

This chapter highlights possibly the most important board function of all: setting the direction for the enterprise, or answering the question: Where are we going? To be absolutely clear, setting strategic direction is a board prerogative not restricted to management alone. However, implementation of the policies established by the board is clearly in the domain of management. It is, therefore, essential that the senior management team, led by the chief executive officer, be an integral part of the planning process. This is necessary not only because management possesses the logistical resources to establish the details of the future corporate direction, commonly known as the strategic plan, but because without total management commitment, successful implementation of any plan will be in jeopardy.

Many board chairmen look on the strategic planning process as analogous to an annual medical checkup, a clean bill of health that evaluates every aspect of the company. The process involves examining the very style of the company's operation, the development of management, as well as the achievement of profits. It delves into potential threats to the company's existence which, if left unchecked, could engender a period of severe ill health that, in the extreme, can be terminal. It also alerts the board to opportunities that, if properly and responsibly exploited, can improve greatly the future prognosis.

BOARD INVOLVEMENT IN THE PROCESS

Until recently, a strong body of opinion held that the strategic plan was owned by management and the board simply approved it. This idea may have been a function of ignorance of where the real responsibility lay, perhaps because strong CEOs felt that this was their domain and not the board's or also because very few boards were primed as to the pivotal role they should play in the process.

This is not to say that every enterprise has to follow an identical pattern. Each organization should be flexible enough to establish its own process as it sees fit. What is a fundamental in developing corporate strategy is a "Royal Road," which consists of:

- Determination of precise objectives according to a specified time frame. What is it that we are trying to achieve and how long should it take us to get there?
- A SWOT analysis—a determination of strengths and weakness internal to the organization and identification of opportunities and threats external to it. These analyses sometimes are identified as position audits and environmental audits respectively. Together both audits respond to the question: Where are we, as an enterprise, today?
- Development of the most effective strategy for getting from "where we are" to "where we want to be." Here strategic thinking, which is discussed in the next section, plays an important role.
- Preparation of a clear-cut plan to achieve the strategic objectives, showing the changes necessary in the marketing, production, and use of resources in terms of capital, management, human resources, and physical assets, including intellectual property.
- Finally, implementation of the plan with regular board oversight. While the implementation process should not attempt to

change the plan lightly, it should be flexible enough to react to the unexpected. This integral element of risk management is dealt with elsewhere. However, in the context of the strategic plan, the board should be prepared to consider any event that may have a significant impact on its outcome.

One of the most frequent questions asked is for how long a plan should be prepared and how often it should be updated. Frankly, the answers depend on the type of business involved. Retail enterprises find it difficult to forecast more than two or three years into the future, whereas capital-intensive industries would be imprudent if they did not attempt to project up to seven years or more. Five years is a good compromise, with one year being dropped off each year and a new one added. A final caveat: It is considered good practice to revisit the basic goals and objectives and renew the audit process from a zero base if not annually, then at least every two or three years, depending on circumstances.

The board must always, with no exceptions, be involved in developing corporate vision and strategic direction. Although management at several levels should be encouraged to participate, corporate vision is a board-driven process, one in which the collective talent that has been recruited to the board has a positive and pragmatic role to play. The chairman must guide and maintain a strong leadership role, if necessary acting as a foil for an ambitious CEO.

Smaller enterprises with limited management resources should consider using management consultancy talent on a limited objective basis to assist in formulating the actual plan and undertaking the detailed planning process. At this microplanning stage, board involvement should normally be limited but not entirely absent. Judicious involvement by directors often can maintain the broader view so necessary in considering strategic intentions.

Identifying corporate objectives should be a joint effort between management and the board. The CEO has a focal role to play in harmonizing talents.

Approving the overall plan and direction is a board prerogative once again. The CEO must not only carry the board in approving the plan's implementation but also must ensure that the management team is committed to its achievement. The CEO also will be responsible for preparing regular progress reports that measure achievement against the plan and for recommending for board approval any corrective actions that may be required.

DEVELOPING STRATEGIC THINKING

Few books have been written on strategic thinking, although one—
Strategic Thinking—A Step-by-Step Approach to Strategy, by Simon Wootton
and Terry Horne—has a useful extract that defines it (see Exhibit 5.1).

Strategic thinking is the process by which those who provide an enterprise with its direction can rise above normal processes to gain a
better perspective on those factors causing change in their operating
environment. This approach must look both forward and backward so
that risks can be appreciated and understood and repetition of past
mishaps can be avoided. Some, particularly Henry Mintzberg in his
book *The Rise and Fall of Strategic Planning* (see Chapter 9), would have
us believe that strategic planning is an oxymoron, but we will not dwell
on semantics. What most do agree on is that planning is a process that
takes place after strategic thinking.

Exhibit 5.1   Strategic Thinking.

- *Think analytically* about the likely impact of technology, economics, markets, politics, law, ethics and social trends;
- *Think numerically* when carrying out an audit of strategic capability;
- *Think reflectively* about problems and responsibilities;
- *Think predictively* when forecasting the future;
- *Think imaginatively* when writing a mission statement;
- *Think visually* about ways to realise the mission statement;
- *Think creatively* about how to remove obstacles and avoid pitfalls;
- *Think critically* when evaluating the economics, efficiency, effectiveness, feasibility and the risks of available options;
- *Think empathetically* about the consequences for individuals;
- *Think ethically* about the social and environmental implications;
- *Think pragmatically* when writing a plan to manage the changes;
- *Think politically* about obtaining the support of key stakeholders and decision-makers, when implementing the plan.

Source: Adapted from Simon Wootten and Terry Horne, *Strategic Thinking—A Step-by-Step Approach to Strategy* (Kogan Page, 2000), p. iv.

Some also criticize the rigorous analytical approach advocated as being too corporately concentrated, as if the company is the "center of the universe." Others state that strategic energies always must be directed at "reinventing the company." Kenichi Ohmae, the well-known Japanese futurist writing about his country's business strategies in *The Mind of the Strategist* states: "They have an idiosyncratic mode of thinking in which the company, customers, and competition merge in a dynamic interaction out of which a comprehensive set of objectives and plans for action eventually crystallize."[1] In other words, one cannot devise a strategy nor think strategically without taking into account the strategies of current and potential competitors and potential collaborators. And one not only needs to know the end product but also must have a pretty good idea of their respective strengths and vulnerabilities of the foregoing. To quote Bob Garratt in *Developing Strategic Thought*:

> Now we can see that, at the higher levels of board thinking, the whole enterprise is put in the context of the overall business situation. Thinking encapsulates past experiences, current information and expectations about the foreseeable future. It is an ongoing process, not the creation of a specific plan. Strategy formulation is idiosyncratic, emergent, non-linear and provides guidance to the ongoing activities of the enterprise.[2]

GOALS AND OBJECTIVES

Thus far we have blended the analytical with the creative approach, both of which are essential constituents in setting the direction. As stated, the board plays a fundamental role in establishing goals and objectives for the corporation. It is, of course, explicitly understood that the CEO and management must be involved, not only by virtue of their intimate knowledge of the activities of the enterprise but also to ensure their wholehearted commitment in the implementation of the plan when it is finalized.

Many companies tend to look upon setting goals and objectives as subjective, to the extent that they have "wish lists" without any specific targets and results in mind. This may be fine for the expansive brainstorming activity that comes a little later, but it is important not to lose sight of where the company wishes to go. Vague goals, such as "to be the best in the world at . . ." are laudable, but what do they really mean? It is necessary to go one stage further to translate such wishes into authentic objectives.

Similarly, merely setting numerical goals without relating them to strategic targets is also of limited value. Achieving sales of x with a net profit of y by year z may be an eventual outcome, but the rationale for arriving at these figures must be explained fully.

Many companies try to set too many objectives. Often they are going into too great detail at too early a stage. Consider the objective-setting process as a pyramid from the top down. As progressively more detail is abstracted, it will become much clearer what resources will be required. Invariably, there will be competition for such resources, usually financial but very often human, particularly management resources.

Consider one organization strategizing where it wished to be in five years' time and setting financial goals. In calculating what it would take to achieve these goals, it became clear that the 14 top managers sitting around the table would require to be increased to something like 37—all in 5 short years. Most of the participants thought this was very amusing and far-fetched, until it was explained in detail what, in this case, too rapid an expansion would require and whether it would be feasible, or responsible, to attempt it.

The principle of iteration is commonly used in the strategic planning process to recalculate the requirements of a set of goals and objectives until a satisfactory fit is achieved with the resources likely to become available.

Some organizations tend to confuse the words "vision" and "mission" with the strategy formulation process. Both vision and mission are rather more fundamental and, ideally, should be considered separately, prior to formulating the strategic plan. Establishing a corporate vision is analogous to guiding an organization through the fog. The rapid changes in technology forced on companies in recent years have not simplified the process. A vision, basically, is the distillation of a collection of beliefs harnessed to the future direction of the organization. One author likens it to playing chess rather than roulette.

A mission statement should be regarded as the organizing principle, something that gets one's attention, is simple and understandable. To be understood by everyone from the very top to the very bottom of an organization is a challenge, but the best mission statements are not constructed in a vacuum. They are constructed so as to relate, in simple language, why the organization exists, what it stands for, and what it plans to achieve. The Disney organization, for example, has chosen the elegant mission statement "To make people happy."

In summary, the corporate goals and objectives must be few in number, realistic, tangible, easily understood, and potentially attainable.

THE ROLE OF MANAGEMENT

As discussed, the board plays a major role in setting the direction of the enterprise. It must be substantially involved in the strategy planning process, a process that, in the past, tended to be dominated by management. The board does not displace management's participation, rather it enhances it. Directors, almost by definition, are expected to bring a much broader perspective to the company. They have diverse skills and expertise. They add the macroscopic rather than a microscopic dimension.

Management, however, has the necessary skills to make the plan happen. It tends to know, perhaps often instinctively, whether something is feasible and achievable. Managers may even know the major risks of implementation. Traditionally, however, management tends to be over-optimistic. This optimism relates partly to pride, which is understandable, and partly to protection of one's territory or status. The board must not frustrate genuine initiative but must temper it with reality. Challenge must be carefully structured so as to be constructive in this part of the process.

This brings about the problem of competition for resources. Experience has shown that, apart from financial constraints, the availability of suitably competent people is often a major limiting factor. In deciding who should be allowed to do what, and when, the board often must balance competing proposals.

The management team, under the careful guidance of the CEO, prepares the backup materials for the various audits—the SWOT analysis. Subsequently it prepares documentation, progressively more detailed, for the selected scenarios, iterating if need be to ensure the most effective use of resources and the most responsible attitudes toward risk.

Forward planning involves an excursion into the unknown. A number of important management tools exist (see Chapter 9) that can help in assessing risk and the probabilities of certain events occurring. While they are not precise, such devices help to evaluate the relative importance of various risk factors so that management and the board can become aware of which elements of the strategic plan are the most critical. Rank ordering these elements dictates where the greatest prudence in planning and the most careful monitoring during implementation should take place.

Finally, once the overall basis of the strategic plan is agreed, it is the responsibility of the management team to prepare the working documents so that implementation can move forward. The team must calculate more detailed projections that become the controls against which performance is measured.

MAINTAINING OVERSIGHT

A corporate strategic plan must be sufficiently specific to provide a rubric for implementation. However, the more specific a plan is, the more it can restrict the company's flexibility to react to the unanticipated. Sticking to a plan, or parts of it, that has become obsolete by changed circumstances can be as restrictive as using quill pens instead of a computer. No plan should ever be cast in stone. A plan can only be as good as circumstances at the time it was prepared allow it to be.

However, a plan provides a datum against which progress can be measured. Remove the datum, and focus is lost—a situation analogous to losing one's bearings. Therefore, simply because actual performance measured against the plan varies does not, in itself, provide justification for change. Two other criteria must be taken into consideration.

1. Have the underlying assumptions on which the plan (or a significant part of it) were based changed materially? This must be true to the extent that, almost by definition, they invalidate the basic parameters on which the plan was constructed. Board members must be heavily involved in responding to this question because they alone can preserve the vital objectivity necessary. Management may recommend, but the board must approve.
2. Have the changes that have occurred introduced elements of business risk that previously were considered acceptable but now are not? In other words, even though the plan may remain essentially valid, are the assumptions on which it was drawn up now so much riskier that alternative strategies should be considered? The meltdown in the high-tech sector in late 2000 to early 2001 is a case in point; previously prudent policies became imprudent quite rapidly because of a combination of circumstances. While the meltdown in the economic situation may have been predicted, in a competitive environment, timing is of the essence.

In some cases these changes in circumstances could not reasonably have been foreseen (although one could argue that prudent use of the modeling techniques of probability analysis and stochastic decision trees [see Chapter 9] may have identified areas of greater potential vulnerability). However, once it began to become apparent that major structural change was occurring in the marketplace, prudent and perceptive enterprises should have immediately reviewed where they intended to go.

According to management consultant David Hargreaves:

> So far, corporate [strategic] planning may well have appeared logical, probably useful, and certainly harmless. It is not as easy as that. Quite apart from the actual planning problems—especially in comparative evaluation—the existence of a plan poses management problems. . . . While a plan is a bad master, it is an excellent servant. The man who knows exactly where his company stands, what it ought to do, what it is capable of doing, and where it is going, is in a much better position than the man who has no such plan to take a risk that is carefully calculated, rather than a "fingers crossed" leap in the dark. . . . [I]f the plan is regarded as a corporate Bible, it must be used as a signpost, not as a strait-jacket.[3]

Assuming that the direction that the board has set for the enterprise remains valid, then two things must occur:

1. The board should be provided with a regular (three-monthly is an ideal interval) update of progress in the implementation of the plan. Remember, the strategic plan is not an operational document in itself. Specific operational budgets prepared from the plan provide these details. The report must list any significant variations from the plan and management's intention (and capabilities) to regularize the situation.

2. The board should be alerted to any early warning signs that may have been detected which have altered the risk criteria on which the plan was prepared. Again, since management is closer to the action, it should recommend to the board if any prudent actions or changes should be considered. The management team should focus at least six months to one year ahead so that, at the very least, when the time comes for revising and extending the plan, the board is aware in good time of any material changes to the fundamental planning parameters.

CHAPTER 6

The Minefield of Legal Liability Exposure

In squandering wealth as his particular art;
Nothing went unrewarded, but desert,
Beggar'd by fools, whom still he found too late
He had his jest, and they had his estate.

—John Dryden, *Absalom and Achitopel.*

In today's litigious climate, the chairman of the board and all board members must behave in a diligent manner. Chapter 4 outlined the breadth of liability facing a director of an incorporated enterprise. This chapter highlights the type of board behavior and practice that can reduce the likelihood of falling afoul of the law or other regulatory constraints. Prudent and diligent behavior on the part of directors can help to steer a company clear of difficult situations.

This chapter details a case in which several major financial institutions sued an entire board for alleged misrepresentation. The fact that it could be argued that the institutions involved should have been sufficiently sophisticated in their procedures to ensure that misrepresentation could not occur was irrelevant to the case. The institutions had deep pockets, much deeper than the directors concerned, which placed the latter in financial jeopardy even to defend the suit against them—

whether the suit had merits or not. Fortunately, liability insurance remained in force and covered substantially all of the costs. But it need not have covered most costs. The total amount claimed was eight times the value of the insurance coverage and the writs were issued a matter of only days before the policy coverage was due to expire. In this instance chance (and maybe a little luck) was on the side of the defendants.

INTERPRETING THE SITUATION

Many directors have expressed concern that, in this day and age of technological change, it is impossible, or perhaps not practical, for them to know everything that is going on in a company or the extent of potential legal liability. Therefore, how can they be held responsible? There is always a question of degree, and the courts are constantly refining their judgments in an attempt to distinguish between poor corporate governance and genuine, and excusable, lack of knowledge.

Directors who hold multiboard appointments can be particularly at risk since they tend to believe that they bring a degree of special expertise to each board, rather than being, quoting medical terminology, a general practitioner.

Unfortunately, the law does not easily distinguish between different types of directors (although recent cases sometimes have held directors with specialized knowledge to a higher standard than those without it). They are all considered equal, and equally legally exposed. However—and this is an important point—if directors, either individually or collectively, make discerning inquiries and then make independent judgments, they likely will have a better chance to prove that they have acted diligently.

As mentioned previously, recently an entire board, indeed anyone who had ever been a director in the company, which ultimately went bankrupt, was sued by a major financial institution for misrepresentation. One director who had resigned well over two years prior to the bankruptcy asked why he was included in the suit. Through legal counsel he was informed that the financial institution claimed to have relied on financial statements prepared during the period of the director's incumbency (as well as those prepared long after his departure).

Not satisfied, the director then proceeded, again through legal counsel, to serve what is known as a motion for summary judgment. This is a device to force a plaintiff to prove to the court that it has a prima facie case against the defendant. As part of the process, the defendant was subjected to cross-examination by the plaintiff's counsel, who promptly proceeded to go through previous board minutes exhaustively. As the inquisition proceeded, it became clear that the director in question had not been a silent observer at board meetings. Far from it. He had consistently questioned actions being taken and probed decisions being requested of the board. Although never openly refuting decisions of the majority, it became apparent that this director had acted diligently, and the chances of the plaintiff making a case against the director were slim. Accordingly, the director was successful in having himself removed from the suit.

Fortunately, the corporate secretary had recorded details of such discussions in sufficient detail that an adequate and consistent paper trail had been established. This trail was a crucial key to the process. Many lawyers advocate that directors keep their own notes of discussions taken at board meetings and decisions taken, with particular reference to their own participation. However, there is a potential downside to such a process; should a lawsuit ever occur, plaintiffs can insist on such documentation being produced. The documentation may, or may not, be to the defendant director's benefit. Other lawyers suggest that the procedure should be followed up to the time that the minutes of the meeting have been produced, agreed, and approved, at which point the personal notes may be destroyed. There is no hard and fast rule or advice on this score, other than to ensure that there is some credible substantiation that the diligence process has been pursued.

THE STATUTORY POSITION

To fulfill the statutory requirement of diligence, a director should make those inquiries that a person of ordinary care, in his or her position, or in managing one's own affairs, would make. The common law standard has become the statutory standard and the consequences of breaching it cannot be removed by agreement or bylaw (with one minor exception that will be ignored here).

According to the booklet *Duties and Responsibilities of Directors in Canada*, directors are not bound to attend all meetings of the board, otherwise those who hold multiple directorships might find themselves in difficulty.[1] However, directors ought to attend as many as possible as there is the possibility of being held liable for transactions about which they had no prior knowledge. Failure to attend meetings, although not in itself a liability, may be evidence of lack of diligence. One unattributed quotation states: "He cannot say he was ill, too busy, or on too many boards, or on the golf course, at the time the questioned decision was made."

Furthermore, directors cannot shirk their responsibilities by relying on others, in particular codirectors, or on the officers of the company. Directors who rely on others do so at their own risk. They should not rely unquestioningly on codirectors and on the corporation's officers. The general rule is that directors should not be liable for the misdeeds of codirectors where directors have not participated in the acts resulting in the damage and are not personally negligent.

However, many acts under which businesses are incorporated provide little escape in the interpretation of this rule unless the dissent is expressly recorded in writing at the time. Directors remain totally responsible for ensuring that they receive adequate information from management. Directors also should recognize the risk of relying on this source of information and take whatever safeguards considered necessary to verify its accuracy.

For example and at the very minimum, directors should examine the financial statements and review the general business activities with the executive officers of the company. They are not required, or expected, to go behind the entries in the company's books in the absence of suspicious circumstances.

Directors are not expected to be experts in all fields and often must rely on the advice of specialists. In certain circumstances, directors may rely on the advice or opinion of outsiders—in cases in which the outsider is independent of the directors, appears qualified to provide the advice, and the directors still exercise their own judgment.

Furthermore, directors who are on the boards of several companies that may be dealing with one another may be well advised to advocate the retention of separate outside specialist advisors. A word here about the concept of a nominee or "dummy" director. The term sometimes is used to describe a director who is elected (by a separate constituency or shareholder group) on the understanding that he or she is merely to obey orders given by someone else. (Sometimes a majority or substantial majority shareholder is invited to nominate one or more directors to the board as a "deemed" representative of the shareholder.) Being a dummy, nominee, honorary, or part-time director does not lessen one's responsibilities or duties. There is also no distinction between duties and responsibilities of inside executive and outside (independent) directors. Newly appointed directors may be saddled with the sins of their predecessors.

Finally a word about illegal or improper acts. A director who acquires knowledge of an illegal act on the part of codirectors, the board, or the company has a clearly defined course of action—and it is not inaction. Neither may immediate resignation provide total relief. While the director may not be liable for any improper act of the board or the company of which they may have been ignorant, or which may have occurred prior to their becoming a director, when learning of such wrongful act they must take immediate and effective steps to become absolved.

Merely requesting a notation in the minute book is not sufficient. For example, where three of five directors of a subsidiary company became aware of the parent's policy to destroy the subsidiary by diverting business to the parent, and the directors did nothing to save the subsidiary—not even advising their two codirectors—it was held that they were liable for their inaction.

WHEN TO SEEK ADVICE

There are basically three sets of circumstance relating to seeking advice. These circumstances involve different levels of inquiry and, ultimately, concern. The first relates to situations that require explanation. Probably the most common situation facing directors occurs when they are called on to contribute toward making a decision about which they have too little knowledge or information, or possibly insufficient time to make a rational contribution. This was the nub of the criticism leveled against the directors in the Trans Union case (*Smith v. Van Gorkum*) where a shareholder successfully sued the board of Trans Union for accepting a takeover offer that was judged too low. In fact, the court, in a very strongly worded criticism, asserted that certain decisions had been made without the majority of the board having read and/or digested critical information.

Therefore, it is extremely important that briefing papers are circulated well in advance of board meetings and that directors are provided with the opportunity to seek clarification or amplification from the senior officers and/or management of the corporation before as well as during the meeting. In addition, the chairman should be most reluctant to allow items to be placed on the agenda without such opportunities being provided. Many chairmen, in fact, insist that they review the agenda a significant time in advance of proposed board meetings to ensure that adequate briefing materials are made available.

In a contingency situation, shortcuts are inevitable. In such circumstances, the chairman and chief executive officer must go out of their way to explain the nature of the emergency and satisfy the outside directors of the prudence of the proposed actions. Emergencies, however, by definition should not occur too often.

The second type of situation involves policy or changes in policy. In these situations, something fundamental, such as a change in strategy, is planned, or something dramatic is about to occur. Examples of the former could be a bid for the company or a takeover offer. Examples of the latter could be the possible resignation of the CEO or a sudden and significant change in financial circumstances.

A board meeting called in such circumstances, even by teleconference, demands much more stringent attention by directors. The legal and financial stakes are much higher than in routine circumstances, and directors must insist that *all* the pertinent facts are placed at their disposal without embellishment. This type of situation often demands the use of outside advisors—legal, financial, or other specialist disciplines as necessary. While exercising thrift and not needlessly committing corporate funds for expensive outside counsel, the board must nevertheless consider very carefully whether it is not only in its best interests, but also in those of the company, to retain such outside advice from time to time.

In many situations in which directors have found themselves criticized or even legally exposed, they have not sought outside advice or not sought it early enough. The board should be very cautious about basing decisions solely on the expertise of a board member, however well qualified. A conflict of interest or even self-interest may be brought into play. Besides, independent verification carries more weight and provides peace of mind.

The last situation involves the law. Most corporations at some time or other become involved in disputes. Invariably, some of these disputes will involve litigation; in the extreme, some may involve criminal proceedings. No company and no director enjoys these types of activities. Even if successfully conducted, the costs may be astronomical in relation to possible benefits. In some instances, though, the corporation and its directors may have little option—they will have to fight.

However, in many situations such exposure can be avoided or at least negotiated to a reasonable degree of compromise. Exposure can be avoided in most cases involving conflicts of interest, contractual obligations, takeovers, mergers, stock prospectuses, and so on. Good advice and due diligence are two major ingredients to be applied in full measure.

DANGER SIGNALS

Much has been made of the danger of rubber stamping and endorsing actions of others by default. Default endorsements include not only acceptance of committee reports and actions implicit within them. In particular, actions of an executive committee that is mandated to meet more frequently than the main board and may, incorrectly, assume some of its responsibilities sometimes pre-empt responsibilities of the full board.

Some boards, on the grounds of expediency and quite inappropriately, produce minutes of "dummy" board meetings purported to have been held some time previously and dated so as to approve particular actions retroactively. Such a practice is out of order. Nevertheless, situations do arise in which resolutions may be prepared in writing and circulated ahead of time for directors' approval, or couriers may be used or electronic means considered if an emergency has arisen. Another alternative that may be considered is to seek a waiver of notice on a timely basis and/or call a meeting of those directors readily available, providing this generates a quorum.

In general, directors must insist on:

- Full and accurate information being provided to them
- Being given sufficient time to seek elaboration and explanation
- Not being pressured either unreasonably or unduly
- Being prepared to approve conditionally but not necessarily unequivocally

The most prevalent sin in many corporations is providing the board with insufficient information, on a historical (rather than current) basis, and too late for any meaningful actions to be taken to correct adverse trends. Possible reasons for this sin may include:

- Less than competent management or an incomplete management structure
- Inadequate information systems
- Lack of planning or budgetary control procedures
- Lack of operating systems and/or diligent supervision

However, directors must be alerted to less evident danger signals. These can include:

- Misguided loyalties in concealing mistakes and inefficiencies
- Excessive pressure on staff members causing problems of morale, absenteeism, or sickness
- Lack of respect for the board and reluctance to submit to its ultimate authority

These are all what may be described as structural indicators of problems within the organization. However, a number of more tangible indicators may provide meaningful evidence to discriminating inquirers that all is not well. Obviously, not all of these may be relevant to any one industry or service:

- Uneven or erratic delivery patterns, stock outs and back orders, returns, complaints regarding customer service
- Employee discontent, staff or labor turnover, work stoppages, excessive complaints, wage anomalies, excessive overtime
- Fluctuating bank balances, uneven payment records, high levels of accounts receivables and payables, erratic record of withholding tax payments (with potential personal liability for directors), uneven sales patterns and order input
- Uneven or unexplained movement in the company's share prices, any movements against market trend, any sudden fluctuations (also an indicator of possible takeover intention)

This list indicates where directors should look for explanations, what questions they should ask of management, and where judgment should be applied in reconciling explanations given and discussing them either at board meetings or with other board members from an informed perspective.

A SENSE OF TRUE PERSPECTIVE

Exercising due diligence involves making sufficient inquiry as if dealing with one's own affairs and then making independent judgment. Perhaps one of the more succinct descriptions is: Fiduciaries [i.e., directors] cannot delegate their discretion or rely on other opinions. They can ask for advice, but must make an independent business decision.

An article reported in the UK *Financial Director*, highlights what it described as a major shift that is occurring in the nature of due diligence: "The traditional attitude of merely making sure all the figures are in order is being replaced by a concern for a wider range of issues. Underlying market forces and commercial fit are now serious considerations."[2]

Chairman Barrie Pearson, of the corporate finance company Livingstone Guarantee, remarked about the corporate acquisition process: "We always get concerned when acquirers appoint investigating accountants to check tax and financial matters, but are prepared to take on trust what the vendors will tell them orally about the commercial well-being and standing of the business. Some companies overlook the underlying market forces that give an insight not only into the achievable results of the next few years but the medium to long-term outlook for that company." Pearson concludes—and bear in mind he is talking primarily about the acquisition process—that "At the end of the day, the aim of due diligence is to quantify the downside. You have to look at it in connection with the strategic relevance of the acquisition. . . . The important thing is that the risks have been identified and financially quantified."[3]

In the same article, Alan Isaacs, national chairman of KPMG in New Zealand, was quoted as saying: "How often have we heard it in the past? A company has gone into receivership and the CEO and the directors blame a downturn in the economy, or high interest rates, as the primary cause of their collapse." Isaacs blames internal deficiencies as the most common reason given for company failures. He suggests that a number of more potent indicators may provide early warning that a company may be heading toward insolvency:

- Negative trends such as recurring operating losses or negative cash flows
- Working capital deficiencies, or a working capital ratio significantly worse than industry norms

- Negative or shrinking shareholders' equity
- Denial by suppliers or bankers of usual credit facilities
- A high debt-to-equity ratio
- Heavy dependency on short-term financing
- Loss of a major customer in a key market
- External factors, such as an industry downturn and/or legislation affecting the ability to trade

Isaacs emphasizes that none of these indicators in itself is necessarily bad, "but each can be a symptom of the three basic causes of business failure: poor management, poor management and poor management!"[4]

From a corporate director's perspective, where does all this dialogue lead? A single word indicates how directors must conduct themselves: proactively. They must always take the initiative. By far, most symptoms or indicators mentioned can be recognized fairly easily. Directors are not expected to be experts in every field of business, not even in the business of the company on whose board they sit. But they are expected to be worldly and to demonstrate a desire to learn and act independently.

Sometimes directors have argued that they are not there to second guess management, nor to micromanage (i.e., to become involved in levels of detail that could be said to encroach on the domain of operational management). These arguments are absolutely correct; directors must refrain from offering advice to management along the lines of "If I were you, I would do . . ." This immediately places them in the arena over which the board is expected to maintain diligent oversight.

However, directors are supposed to retain that broader perspective of business. They must either be aware or make themselves aware of the major threats and opportunities facing the company's business. And if they choose to allow themselves to be informed of these threats and opportunities by management, a judgment to request some independent verification may not be out of place.

Consider, for example, the Report of the South Australian Auditor General after the spectacular collapse of the State Bank of South Australia in 1991. After discussing many failures of management, the auditor general stated:

> . . . the bank's board of directors was, for the most part, ineffective. I have some sympathy for the bank's non-executive (outside) directors. They lacked both banking experience and, in most cases, hard-

headed business acumen. They were manipulated, and not properly informed of what was going on. The information given to them was voluminous, but obscure. It took an expert and practised eye to sort the wheat from the chaff and to know what information was not there. The board lacked that. But whatever sympathy one may have for its predicament, the board of directors was the governing body of the bank, charged with responsibility to administer the bank's affairs and to control the chief executive in performance of his management function. A reasonably prudent board—whatever its skills—would have done much more than the bank's board did. It was not beyond the capabilities of the non-executive directors to take commonsense measures and to stand no nonsense.

To be blunt, there is nothing esoteric about asking questions, seeking information, demanding explanations and extracting further details. There is nothing unduly burdensome in expecting each director, to the best of his or her ability, to insist on understanding what was laid before them, even at the risk of becoming unpopular. Both the law and a basic sense of duty and responsibility demand it. The nonexecutive directors submitted to me that they did these things. Sometimes they did, but not often enough, and not strongly enough. I have repeatedly found that the board of directors failed to adequately or properly supervise, direct and control the operations, affairs and transactions of the bank.[5]

DILIGENCE AND THE STRATEGY PROCESS

Chapter 5 discusses the fact that some directors still feel that it is inappropriate for the board to become involved in the formulation of strategy—that this is a management function. Others indicate that they would be more comfortable with thinking rather than planning strategically. Whichever approach one adopts, there is little doubt that the board has an obligation to maintain diligent oversight. In order to do this, there must be some tangible degree of involvement.

The approach advocated by Charles Anderson and Robert Anthony in *The New Corporate Directors* is perhaps becoming outmoded:

> While it is unrealistic to expect directors to formulate strategy, they should satisfy themselves that management has a sound process for developing it. The strategy is probably acceptable if:
>
> (a) It is based on careful analysis by people who are in the best position to evaluate it, rather than on an inspiration accepted without study;

(b) The reasoning seems sensible, [and we would add that it must be based on responsible analysis];

(c) The directors are not aware of significant information that has been omitted from the analysis; and

(d) The results expected from the strategy are clearly set forth so that actual accomplishment can be compared with them.[6]

The only difficulties with this approach are that directors are expected to be reactive, digest what is often a voluminous amount of information, and understand the underlying thinking behind the presentation. A more modern process dictates that directors actually participate actively in the consideration of overall objectives: Where does the corporation wish to go? Which business(es) should we be in? It is almost axiomatic today that the process is not immutable. Changes must occur as conditions and circumstances change. However, as Anderson and Anthony state: "[C]hanging them [the objectives] requires a more rigorous analysis than does adhering to them."

To summarize: Responsible and effective boards should insist on a distinctive and enduring corporate strategy, one that is regularly reviewed to ensure that it remains valid and used as a benchmark for all other strategic board decisions. Management must also recognize, understand, and accept the risks associated with the adoption of the strategic plan.

Diligence requires:

- Involvement in the formulation of overall objectives
- Insistence on process
- Challenging assumptions
- Constant and regular review

SOME SPECIFIC AREAS OF VULNERABILITY

Directors may ask if there are any areas of specific vulnerability. It is very difficult to generalize, but there has been significant new legislation in recent years as well as increased regulation by some statutory authorities.

The final Report of the Toronto Stock Exchange Committee on Corporate Disclosure (the Allen Report) came out strongly in favor of increasing sanctions against anyone who provides misleading or, by inference, incomplete information. What this means in practice is that issuing companies (i.e., those listed on the Toronto Stock Exchange) have an obligation, which is subject to civil liability, to disclose any information that should be in the public domain. At the time of this writing the report has not been promulgated in any regulations. Suffice to state that directors must assume responsibility for the dissemination of information, its accuracy, and timeliness. One clause in the report makes interesting and potentially onerous reading: "Plaintiffs [i.e., someone alleging misleading disclosure] should not be obliged to prove that they read the misrepresentation or that they relied upon the misrepresentation in making their investment decision. Reliance should be deemed to have occurred." In other words, not only do listed companies have an obligation to issue information, but the liability for its accuracy extends to the company, its officers, and its directors "who authorized, permitted or acquiesced in the issuance of the disclosure, or in a decision not to disclose a material change, when it ought to have been disclosed."[7]

In October 2000, the U.S. Securities and Exchange Commission imposed Regulation Fair Disclosure (FD). It imposes fair, as opposed to selective, disclosure to all investors on an equal basis. It was argued initially that Regulation FD would cause the flow of information to dry up and that news, perhaps unexpected, of negative earnings forecasts would cause severe share market fluctuations. In fact, some criticism for the market downturn and volatility during 2001 has been blamed in part on the increased need for disclosure when news of material importance becomes apparent. However, cooler heads have suggested that economic news and an overheated market, particularly in dot-com companies, have been a more likely source of the problem. What Regulation FD has encouraged is more independent stock analysis and a shift toward focusing on longer- rather than shorter-term potential.

In terms of issuing a prospectus, the various acts require that directors ensure that "an extensive investigation into the affairs of the corporation is conducted, to satisfy themselves that no material fact is misstated in, or omitted from, the prospectus. By doing this, the directors are more likely to be able to insulate themselves from liability, as well as ensuring that the company's risks of exposure are minimized."[8] Parallel obligations arise during the course of a takeover bid, whether making or receiving, as was mentioned in the Trans Union case.

Environmental protection legislation also places a requirement on directors to ensure that the corporation takes a proactive stance in preventing pollution. Furthermore, if a spill or other damage occurs, appropriate steps and legally specified actions must be taken to deal with the situation. Many companies prepare a "Green Plan" and place the responsibility on a senior manager to monitor the situation continuously and report to the board that the plan is being implemented and nothing untoward has occurred or is likely to occur.

Similar constraints are placed on directors in regard to health and safety and under recent labor legislation. Readers are advised to seek specialist advice if exposed to risk in such fields.

Finally, and perhaps looking to the future, note should be made regarding the solvency of a corporation. In some jurisdictions, notably the United Kingdom and Australia, it is an offense for directors to allow a company to continue trading when they know that the corporation is insolvent (and therefore unlikely to be able to pay for debts currently being incurred). Legislation of similar severity has not yet been imposed in Canada or the United States, but not only could it happen, it is sound, indeed ethical, corporate governance not to allow trading while insolvent. In addition, directors should take active steps to prevent insolvency from occurring. Because of the historical nature of financial statements, there is a risk that once information becomes available, the opportunity to take certain remedial actions may have been lost. It is also a distinct possibility that, in a troubled company, information becomes less available because of actual or potential breakdowns in operating procedures and controls. These remarks are intended only to be advisory in nature, but directors would do well to be alert to such possibilities.

HOW MUCH DILIGENCE?

Previous sections have highlighted how directors can be presented with too much information and have difficulty in sifting relevant facts from the less than relevant. Therefore, a useful question to ask is: How much diligence is a director expected to exercise?

In recent years, a significant body of Australian experience has helped to clarify the answers to this question. The following quotations are all extracted from reports quoted by Henry Bosch in *The Director at Risk*.[9] However, readers should not forget that the North American business landscape has also been littered with financial sector collapses in recent years including, but not confined to: the Canadian Commercial Bank and Northland Bank (both subjects of the Estey Enquiry), Standard Trustco, Central Guaranty Trust, Confederation Life Insurance Company, and, of course, more recently Waste Management and Enron. In every instance the directors were or are likely to be indicted. Unfortunately few specific judgments have been rendered that could allow us to define the statutes with greater accuracy.

The report of the Australian Royal Commission into a merchant bank called Tricontinental quoted this about the chief executive officer: "He elected to perform his task as if the merchant bank was his personal property. He kept far too many of the day to day activities of the bank under his personal control. He treated his board of directors as a group of men to be placated and manipulated. . . . He ensured that there were no checks and balances which would inhibit him. . . . He made reckless decisions on inadequate information." The board, which had the power to remove him and the responsibility to ensure that the bank was being managed properly, allowed the situation to continue to the point of disaster. Situations with some similarities have arisen in North America as well.

In the Australian AWA case, Mr. Justice Rogers stated (somewhat surprisingly) that a director is justified in trusting officers and in relying without verification on their judgment, information, and advice: "A non-executive director does not have to turn himself into an auditor, managing director, chairman or other officer to find out whether management are deceiving him."[10] But, as Bosch states, " . . .[such] words present a considerable temptation to directors to sit back and relax, leave it all to management, but such a reaction would not be wise."[11]

So perhaps we should leave the last words to the Australian Royal Commission in the Tricontinental case referred to earlier:

> . . . a board should ensure that it retains effective control over management, whatever the size of the corporation. To do that there must be workable systems which result in the board monitoring accurately the operations of the corporation. It is not enough merely to pronounce upon policy. There is a need to be satisfied properly that the policy is being implemented fully and efficiently. To put the matter at its simplest, the board needs to know what is really going on, and that requires more than formal reports from a chief executive officer. It would be absolutely wrong, in a major public corporation, for the board to permit the chief executive officer to be a one man band. The board must retain effective control, but with that, of course, comes corresponding responsibility and accountability.[12]

ASSUMPTION OF RISK

No book on the role of the board chairman would be complete without some discussion on the subject of risk. Many boards consider risk part of the normal business process. Far from it. Risk is a much broader topic, and its tentacles extend far beyond what most boards would consider normal.

The United Kingdom has instituted what may be the most far-reaching mechanisms for dealing with business risk. The original report of the Hampel Committee (as adopted by the London Stock Exchange for all listed companies) set out three core principles of internal control that must be instituted and maintained for listed companies:

1. Present a balanced and understandable assessment of the company's position and prospects
2. Maintain a sound system of internal control to safeguard shareholders' investment and the company's assets
3. Establish formal and transparent arrangements for considering how the financial reporting and control principles should be applied[13]

The Turnbull report of the Institute of Chartered Accountants in England and Wales specified necessary internal control requirements. A company's internal control system should:

- Be embedded within its operations and not be treated as a separate exercise
- Be able to respond to changing risks within and outside the company
- Enable each company to apply it in an appropriate manner related to its key risks[14]

The U.S. office of the accounting firm KPMG published a booklet in 1999 entitled "Shaping the Audit Committee Agenda." It examined current issues and risks "which we believe should be on every audit committee's agenda." Thus far this text has not examined the role of the audit committee or any other board committee. This is reserved for Chapter 7. However, it is assumed that the oversight of risk management will be undertaken by the audit committee or, increasingly, a purpose-established risk management committee (to relieve the audit committee of potential overload). The committee is being asked to understand and handle every conceivable aspect of business risk. The board chairman is, or should be, intimately involved with all aspects of the operations of these committees and must ensure that their key deliberations are reported regularly, and fully, to the board as a whole.

Patrick Caragata in his excellent book entitled *Business Early Warning Systems* sets out a table shown in Exhibit 6.1 of what he describes as common perils. As he states: "A list like this provides a useful starting point but will probably need to be expanded to include other perils that may be specific to the organization, its business goals, the envi-

Exhibit 6.1   Common Perils.

Contamination	Infestation, Pollution, Water Damage
Denial of Access	Civil Strife and Emergency, Consents, Injunctions, Licenses, Political Unrest, Strikes/Industrial Action, Trade Restrictions, War
Financial	Cash Management, Commodity Trading Prices, Cost and Availability of Finance, Credit Risk, Exchange Risk, Investment Risk
Fire/Explosion	Fire Damage, Explosion, Smoke Contamination
Liability-Common Law	Breach of Confidentiality, Breach of Copyright, Breach of Trust, Claims of Negligence against Directors and Officers, Employee and Third Party Injury, Libel/Slander, Personal Grievance, Product Tamper, Third Party Damage & Disruption
Liability-Contractual	Contracts Obligations (general), Express/Implied Warranty, Failure to Supply
Liability-Statutory	Legislation Imposing Strict Liability on Directors, Officers and Employees, Other Legislation
Loss of Supply	Control Systems, Management Support Systems (e.g. Information Systems),

Exhibit 6.1 *(Continued)*

	Production Equipment, Raw Materials, Skills, Utilities.
Malicious Intent	Espionage, Fraud, Kidnap/Ransom/Extortion, Malicious Damage, Sabotage, Theft
Market Risks	Changes in Fashions & Trends, Costs vs. Pricing, Customer Stability, Fluctuating Economic Conditions, New and Changing Competitors, New Information, New Technology, Regulatory Change, Reputation
Natural Hazards	Forest Fires, Drought, Earthquake, Flood, Land Instability, Lightning, Storm (wind, hail, rain, snow), Temperature Variation, Tornado
Personnel Risks	Employment Contracts, Industrial Relations, Injury and Rehabilitation, Loss of Institutional Knowledge, Loss of Intellectual Property, Skills Dependency
Political Risk	Litigious Markets, Nationalization, Regulations, Sanctions/Embargoes, Tariffs, Duties and Taxes

Source: Patrick J. Caragata, *Business Early Warning Systems* (Butterworth [New Zealand], 1999), p. 125.

ronment in which it operates and the way it goes about conducting its business if a truly comprehensive view is to be taken."[15]

While it is obviously the task of management to be able to recognize and control such risks, the board must play a vital and crucial role in maintaining a strict oversight of the situation. The list is so vast and all-embracing that an efficient and effective system of internal control should be put in place. Kevin Brown, industry editor of the London *Financial Times*, suggests that an efficient system of internal controls should include:

- An explicit statement of risk management expectations, so that managers are clear about what is expected of them

- A clear explanation of the roles and responsibilities of all key players involved in the identification, evaluation, monitoring, and reporting of risk
- A link between risk and business objectives—this will help focus minds and minimize the possibility of significant risks being overlooked
- Formal identification of performance risks, coupled with a board demonstration that it is aware of what the risks are
- Examination of the probability and cost of each possible risk
- Risk-management performance monitoring, which should be carried out periodically
- Shared ethical values [which] need to be established, and authority, responsibility, and accountability [which] must be clearly defined to support the flow of information between people[16]

According to Brown, companies should assess how they currently manage risk before they embark on a program of change. In that way, they will be able to establish and codify existing practices, rather than risk "throwing the baby out with the bathwater."

CHAPTER 7

Delegation—The Use of Board Committees

The act of delegation: To assign responsibility (and commensurate authority) while retaining ultimate accountability.

THE BOARD REMAINS ACCOUNTABLE

President Harry S. Truman uttered the famous words "The buck stops here" to define the ultimate responsibility that he held as head of the executive branch of the U.S. government. He accepted this onerous obligation as he realized there was no higher power to which he could assign blame.

The definition at the beginning of this chapter is an important one. Delegation undoubtedly assigns responsibility, but responsibility is useless without the assignment of sufficient authority to be able to deliver what is required. Similarly, delegation never allows one to relinquish the ultimate responsibility. The chicken invariably comes home to roost.

The board of directors establishes policy. Operational management under the chief executive officer is responsible for its implementation. The board retains the ultimate oversight for performance. However, in today's complex and litigious business environment, the board agenda is usually too large for everything to be dealt with in plenary session. Hence the need to establish committees. These committees do not remove any director from the need to be kept informed.

They are formed to help the board perform its duties more efficiently by dividing the workload. They are not formed to permit the board to infringe on the responsibilities of management.

Nothing is more important than ensuring the proper direction of the enterprise and monitoring progress in achieving its objectives. To facilitate their work, most boards are organized into committees that undertake detailed assessments and evaluations of various tasks and responsibilities. Sometimes work of a more sensitive nature is best handled, at least initially, by a committee rather than by the full board; sensitive areas cover remuneration of senior executives, oversight of internal control procedures, assessment of risk, recruitment of new directors, and dealing with management succession, among other things.

It is also more practicable to work with senior management using the committee structure. Because they are smaller, committees often are less formal and allow presentations and subsequent questions to be less intimidating to the persons concerned. Committees also allow for problems to be worked through and, in cases in which management proposals are likely to be challenged, revisions to be made.

In the end, all committees must report to the full board, and any director has the right to seek clarification to achieve the necessary consensus in decision making. One word of warning: Some committees find it difficult to maintain a balance between invading the delegated area of management and remaining evaluative in their board role. Sometimes committee chairs and key members see themselves as conducting a crusade, which may lead to the development of a counterculture. Outside directors should delve into the operational aspects only to the degree necessary to perform in a diligent manner. Some boards see it as a benefit to use their outside directors as mentors and counselors to management. In these circumstances, it should be clear that the directors are now acting in an advisory capacity and not wearing their governance hat.

In his chapter "Hey, Committees Aren't All That Bad" Ralph Ward writes:

Perhaps the most underreported change in how boards function is the increased use of board committees as working bodies. The greater specialization and intricacy of modern board work is one reason for this. Boards that once nodded their heads and approved what was placed before them could afford interchangeable directors. With more diverse, specialized membership, more technical demands, and limited time, it makes more sense to break tasks down to their components at the committee level. Further, legal, regulatory, and accounting mandates over the years have set high independence standards for board committees. When we add growing concerns over board interlocks, it's wisest to have people with "Caesar's wife" unimpeachability on most committees.

No longer legal niceties, board committees are becoming power centers in their own right. As the board faces new demands, the committee system is proving versatile. Although some new committees are showing up with such concerns as governance, compliance and corporate [social] responsibility, many new board tasks are being taken on by the current committee structure, particularly the audit, nominating, and compensation committees. Why?[1]

SPREADING THE LOAD

All committees should be formed for a specific and valid purpose with their terms of reference clearly stated. Modern practice dictates that the purpose should be stated in a formal manner—in writing. In establishing committees, care should be taken that there is no overlap or redundancy between committees or their agendas. Membership of committees must be chosen carefully so that there is a blend of essential expertise. It is desirable to set up a process of succession whereby, over time, carefully planned rotation occurs. In this manner, ideas do not become stale, traditions do not become engraved in stone, and board members have an opportunity to experience as many facets of board governance as practicable.

Boards must beware of the temptation to form extra committees after the basic few are created. Committees should not be created merely to remove debate from the board agenda. Committees should be used to help the board do its work. Sometimes a difficulty may be too sensitive to be aired initially at a board meeting; the ability to deflect the discussion to a committee may allow an appropriate solution to emerge more easily. This use of committees has the added advantage of allowing the board to focus more on strategic issues. However, the board should differentiate between a formally established committee and an ad hoc task force. The latter is charged with a specific, usually time-limited, mandate; when this goal is achieved, the task force is discharged.

The audit committee usually is, by legal definition, mandatory. All listed companies must have an audit committee; private companies and large not-for-profit organizations should consider having one. A majority, if not all, of an audit committee's members should consist of outside independent directors. All members must be competent in financial literacy. Indeed, legislation in many jurisdictions now demands it.

Many regulated enterprises, such as financial institutions and banks, have other committees mandated by law, such as a conduct review committee, which is charged with maintaining oversight over all major financial commitments the institution enters into.

New committee members should be provided with a comprehensive orientation as, without this, time and director resources do not always allow the privilege of becoming effective over a protracted period. Board committees should be provided with staff resources, where necessary, to assist them in their agenda. Minutes should be recorded in the usual manner (and be made available to all board members as necessary), although in some instances it may be advantageous to summarize them for wider consumption, particularly when dealing with sensitive matters.

Invariably, there are caveats in establishing a committee system and integrating it with the overall work of the board. Leighton and Thain express one such warning well:

> Many boards today have become captive to management, through management's control over the quantity and quality of information provided to the board on strategic issues. Board decisions can only be as good as the information on which they are based. Presentation of biassed data and omission of key facts can decidedly skew board decisions.
>
> Under the growing pressure for performance, boards today are increasingly taking control over their own information systems. Recognising the need for broader, more timely and objective data, boards and board committees are insisting on the right to go beyond the data provided by management to supplement their information, including the use of electronic-based information systems. This makes sense: the kind of information required by a director is often quite different from that normally available to and provided by managers to the board.[2]

Both authors were successful in blending achievement in the academic field with considerable hands-on experience at the board level, often with major corporations. They may be expressing a particularly potent opinion, but it does raise the concern that directors are today held to much higher standards of performance, particularly in regard to diligence, than was formerly the case.

KEY BOARD COMMITTEES

Audit Committee

We have already mentioned the audit committee, often considered by far the most important board committee. As recently as the mid-1980s, an audit committee was considered a relatively new concept. Now it is a universal. It was established initially to work directly with the company's independent auditors, but recently its responsibilities have been expanded substantially. Its primary role is to monitor financial reporting and risk.

In 1999, the U.S. National Association of Corporate Directors published a Blue Ribbon Commission report entitled *Audit Committees: A Practical Guide*, considered one of the finest recent publications of its kind. We quote from the foreword by the commission chairman, A. A. Sommer, Jr.

- The audit committee should focus its attention and tailor its responsibilities appropriately, according to the company's specific environment. Audit committee members should not be overloaded with tasks or they may lose sight of the big picture.
- The ultimate governance body in any corporation is the board of directors. The role of the audit committee cannot, and should not, be allowed to supersede that of the board.
- Without the explicit support of the entire board and management, the audit committee will have difficulty being fully effective.
- A good audit committee is not a cure-all and cannot guarantee prevention of fraud or failure.[3]

Audit committees commonly have three to five members. As mentioned, it is essential that they be financially literate. An inability to understand and interpret financial statements places members at a distinct disadvantage. Directors with accounting qualifications often find themselves drafted onto audit committees, although there have been discussions as to whether audit committees should contain professionally qualified members. Sound business knowledge and comfort in financial matters are often sufficient criteria. Directors should be selected not only because they may make good audit committee members, but because of their qualities as directors, particularly their independence. Key attributes include:

- The ability to ask the right questions at the right time
- Keen analytical skills
- Motivation
- Persistence

This is not the place for a lengthy discussion of the functions and operation of the audit committee. *Audit Committees: A Practical Guide* sums up requirements nicely:

The committee should review and assess:

- Risk Management—including the adequacy of the company's overall control environment.
- Annual Reports and Other Major Regulatory Filings.
- Internal Control and Regulatory Compliance—for detecting and reporting financial errors, fraud and defalcations, legal violations and noncompliance with the corporate code of conduct.
- Regulatory Examinations—the results of examinations by regulatory authorities in terms of important findings, recommendations and management's response.
- External Audit Responsibilities—including the overall scope and focus of the annual and interim audits.
- Financial Reporting and Controls—including key financial statements issues and risks, their impact or potential effect on reported financial information, the processes used by management to address such matters, related auditor views and the basis for audit conclusions.
- Auditor Recommendations—important internal and external auditor recommendations of financial reporting, controls, other matters and management's response.
- Changes in important accounting principles and application thereof.
- Significant conflicts of interest and related-party transactions.
- Internal auditor performance and that of key financial management.
- External auditor performance and changes in external audit firm (subject to ratification by full board).[4]

Some audit committees are delegated the responsibility to analyze and monitor risk. This responsibility has gained increased attention due to the Turnbull Report issued in the United Kingdom and the

Report of the Saucier Committee in Canada.[5] One school of thought promotes the concept of a separately founded risk committee, with the intention of focusing the board's attention on the many aspects of corporate risk (see Chapter 6). Where there is a possibility of overloading the audit committee with too many responsibilities, this idea may be worthy of consideration.

Compensation Committee

John M. Nash, founding president emeritus of the National Association of Corporate Directors, is quoted as saying:

> In the 1980s, the primary focal point of board concern related to audit committee issues . . . In the 1990s, the compensation committee is dealing with the most urgent governance issues. . . . Boards of directors, especially compensation committees, must hold managers accountable and see that they share the risk as well as the reward for their performance. All the shareholders want is a level playing field.[6]

According to the American Bar Association:

> Executive compensation has become *the* issue of discussion in today's corporate governance debate. . . . The executive compensation debate revolves around four questions:
>
> 1. Are the CEO and other senior executives paid too much?
> 2. Is their compensation reasonable related to personal and corporate performance?
> 3. Are the post-employment benefits properly related to the overall benefit of the corporation and reasonable in amount?
> 4. Is there effective oversight of management's compensation?
>
> The compensation committee is at the center of that debate. When functioning responsibly, it not only addresses the first three questions, but also provides credibility and substance to the concept of independent and effective oversight.[7]

These quotes indicate that the whole spectrum of management, and indeed director, compensation is replete with obstacles and challenges, many of which are real but some of which can be perceived as emotional.

Today many boards tend to group activities under the committee structure as governance becomes more complex. Often the whole sphere of the oversight of human resources is allied with compensation. While compensation is possibly the greatest of its challenges, compensation and human resources committees often embrace a significantly wider proportion of the internal, and perhaps more sensitive, activities of the enterprise.

A word here about the concept of remuneration drift. "Drift" denotes the inexorable upward spiral when one attempts to draw a parallel from comparisons with others. Annual reports or proxy circulars often include comments similar to this one:

> The CEO's compensation is determined according to the same compensation policy that applies to other senior officers of the company. Accordingly, the CEO's base salary reflects the median value of similar positions in similar companies in the same industry as well as his level of competency and contribution to the success of the company. The rest of the CEO's compensation is mostly delivered through incentive compensation with particular emphasis on long-term incentive to promote creation of shareholder value.

Four comments can be made here:

1. Comparisons with medians are rarely adhered to. No one wants to be classed as median or average. Therefore, compensation committees may commission surveys or access other comparative information and then decide that the CEO needs some encouragement to remain with the company. To do so, they classify the CEO as being somewhat better than the comparisons. And so the upward spiral continues.
2. Incentives must be meaningful. Rewarding someone for performance that had relatively little to do with ability but more likely circumstance is likely to be counterproductive. One should carefully try to focus incentive on true added value rather than an oversimplistic indicator such as increased share price. At the same time, a CEO who achieves truly positive results in conditions of adversity may deserve a higher reward than one who is operating in smoother waters.
3. Be cautious about nominating directors to the compensation committee where there could be potential conflict of interest. A fellow CEO or senior executive of another company sitting as a director may be chary about being hard-nosed in times of poor operating results. This may possibly reflect more of an

emotional type of empathy with the persons whose remuneration they are considering.

4. Be cautious in allocating corporate stock or stock options. As these often have little real value when awarded, sometimes the temptation is to overallocate to the extent that the shares of the real risk takers, the shareholders who have invested in the company, may be unnecessarily and perhaps unfairly diluted. At least one of the major pension funds is now pursuing a much firmer policy regarding the options in using their proxy voting power at the annual general meetings of companies in which they invest.

The task of the compensation and human resources committee primarily is to monitor the performance, and agree on the remuneration, of top operational management, including the CEO. Such a committee is unlikely to be the most appropriate forum for deciding director compensation; this may best be handled by an ad hoc task force of the board when it becomes necessary.

Recently there has been some considerable outcry over what many consider is excessive executive compensation. In fact, in the United Kingdom, the London Stock Exchange struck the Greenbury Committee, which considered the whole spectrum of senior executive compensation and cautioned against overrewarding, particularly for nonperformance. But perhaps one of the better commentaries was made by Tim Melville-Ross, then director general of the UK Institute of Directors. (The words "senior management" have been substituted for inside or executive directors to reflect differing North American practice.)

> . . . The most important aspect of corporate governance is not senior management rewards; it is helping them create wealth. . . . But unless we tackle it sensibly, confidence in directors and senior management will continue to be undermined. . . . Four pillars support the framework for discussion:
>
> 1. There should be a close link between effort and reward. There is nothing objectionable about substantial rewards for those who take risks and responsibility, innovate and, through their enterprise, create substantial wealth for others.
> 2. There should be no reward for failure, which probably argues against rolling and excessively long fixed-term contracts. It argues for a proper independent mechanism for assessing senior man-

agement performance—itself a case for strong independent director involvement and greater disclosure.

3. Disclosure—openness about reward packages—is central to improving public confidence. Directors in a position of trust and public importance must accept that rewards have to be justified if hostility and suspicion are to be allayed.

4. A much closer link should be established between reward and the long-term performance of the enterprise. This argues strongly for the development of shareholdings and share options as a major element of reward.[8]

James Pitblado, former chairman of RBC Dominion Securities, argued against share options as a free handout, "because there is little risk on the downside." Whatever system is adopted, the overriding criterion must be transparency.

Corporate Governance Committee

In Canada, the corporate governance committee is a relatively new phenomenon arising from the 1994 Toronto Stock Exchange (TSE) Committee's report on corporate governance, *Where Were the Directors?* Its 14 guidelines imposed obligations on listed companies to report their companies' practices. These obligations forced boards to consider a whole raft of issues that hitherto had not usually been part of their agenda and, moreover, to publish a commentary in their annual report (or proxy statement) to shareholders as to how they were complying, or otherwise.

The TSE guidelines include a number of key recommendations. A recent survey published by the TSE, *Five Years to the Dey* (named after Peter Dey, chairman of the original committee), showed very patchy levels of compliance, particularly among medium-size and smaller listed companies. The basic obligations are set out in Guideline 1 of the original report:

The Board of Directors should explicitly assume responsibility for the stewardship of the company including:

(a) adoption of a strategic planning process;

(b) identification of the principal tasks of the company's business, and implementation of the appropriate systems to manage risk;

(c) succession planning, including appointing, training and monitoring senior management;

(d) the company's communications policy;

(e) integrity of the company's internal control and management information systems.

Guideline 4 charges each company to: "Appoint a committee composed exclusively of nonmanagement directors, the majority of which are unrelated [specifically defined in the TSE report], with the responsibility of proposing new board nominees and assessing directors on an ongoing basis."

Guideline 5 requires that the board of directors should: "[I]mplement a process to be carried out by the nominating committee or other appropriate committee for assessing the effectiveness of the board of directors as a whole, the committees of the board and the contribution of individual directors."[9]

Guideline 6 requests each company to provide orientation and education programs for new directors.

The TSE report succeeded in encouraging the empowerment of the board. Prior to its publication, the CEO's influence in securing new directors was pervasive. If the job of CEO and chairman was combined, as it tended to be, then the CEO held a position of even greater power.

The corporate governance committee faces a daunting task, whether unique terms of reference are established for it, or whether it is combined with the nominating or some other committee. For the first time, a specific board committee is charged with reviewing and maintaining oversight of the overall board governance process, including reviewing the board's own performance.

Recent experience indicates that boards and their chairmen are hesitant about becoming involved in anything that may imply criticism. They are uncomfortable in suggesting that the quality of decision making may be less than optimum; that the procedures in place to identify and deal with risk are wanting; indeed, that some members of the board, including possibly the chairman himself, may be performing at lower standards of excellence than may be expected.

For listed companies this situation will surely change; if it does not, regulatory authorities and government eventually could impose ubiquitous controls that will make life much more difficult for the companies. The pressure to improve performance in private enterprise and the not-for-profit sectors, both huge in themselves, is equally manifest.

As this book was being prepared, a new Canadian report on current aspects of corporate governance was published, entitled *Beyond*

Compliance: Building a Governance Culture. Known as the Saucier report after the committee's chairman, Guylaine Saucier, the major findings are to change the emphasis to cultural conformity from structural compliance. However, conformity is still voluntary and time will tell whether listed companies are sufficiently motivated to generate the spirit required by the more demanding levels of corporate governance without regulatory intervention.

Countless annual reports and information circulars of listed companies merely recite the TSE guidelines without providing any substantive information as to *how* they are complying. Such reports are mockeries of what was intended. Peter Dey has stated that the TSE guidelines were introduced when there was a real threat in 1994 that the Canadian government would intercede and impose increased regulation. He maintains that this is still a threat due, in part, to the lack of spirit regarding compliance.

Saucier's committee comes out strongly in favor of disclosure rather than increased regulation. The committee suggests that regulation may be appropriate to enforce certain minimum standards, such as for audit committees, but does not feel that there is any single best model for effective governance. Of interest, however, is the finding that the principles of good governance should apply across the board (no pun intended) to small companies as well as large ones. If a company obtains a public listing and taps into the trough of other people's money, there is every right to hold them equally accountable.

The membership of the corporate governance committee should invariably be drawn from those directors who have the most experience with the company, how it operates, and what direction it wishes to take. Major shareholder interests often desire to provide input as well.

Nominating Committee

Today, the tendency to avoid tokenism and patronage is becoming more prevalent, although retired politicians and public figures still do obtain prestige board appointments. The difference today is that they are more likely to have to work harder on behalf of the company and limit the number of such appointments so that they can devote sufficient of their energies to their board responsibilities. One public figure is reported to have admitted when he assumed his civic responsibilities that he tendered his resignation to a total of 64 boards; no longer would such a situation be possible.

To quote Jim Gillies' *Boardroom Renaissance: Power, Morality and Performance in the Modern Corporation.*

> One can easily see the problems that can arise when a board does not have a nominating committee. Cronyism can take over, friends of friends can become a criteria for board membership and inevitably, without such a committee, the chief executive officer will play a large role in the selection of board members and yet it is one of the major tasks of the board to assess, evaluate and, if necessary, remove management. How can this be done when the members of the board are beholden to management for their appointment in the first place?[10]

Gillies refers readers to Bryan Burrough and John Helyar, *Barbarians at the Gate: The Fall of RJR Nabisco*, for an example of one CEO's shenanigans.[11]

The TSE guidelines suggest that the nominating committee (or some other appropriate committee) assumes responsibility for assessing the effectiveness of the board as a whole and of individual directors. This recommendation is appropriate only if the nominating committee consists of directors with pertinent expertise and, probably equally important, with the correct attitude toward the whole concept of evaluating the performance of the board and individual directors.

Five Years to the Dey showed extremely uneven results in implementing the performance assessment criteria. Not too many consultant organizations have developed appraisal procedures that boards are comfortable in implementing and provide meaningful results against which improvements can be planned and achieved. Some of the earliest systems were extremely rudimentary, requesting directors to respond to simplistic questionnaires with black or white answers. Responses to questionnaires now seek an assessment against a continuum ranging from below to above average; this method allows trends and benchmarks for improvement to be developed. The design of the questionnaire is crucial, as are the instructions for its completion and interpretation (see Chapter 8).

The principal thrust of the nominating committee remains board renewal and succession. Various methods are used to obtain names for consideration to fill board vacancies. Historically the most prevalent has been what Gillies calls the "old boys club." This situation may have worked in the past, particularly for high-profile boards. And it may work today in situations where there are controlling shareholders. It does not seem to work, however, for many of the thousands of corporations that fall into the classification of smaller and medium-size enterprises.

Another tradition that has had its day is the practice of seeking either current or recently retired CEOs from enterprises with similar philosophies. While a similar corporate philosophy is important for maintaining the chemistry of a cohesive board (see Chapter 2), nominating committees should be prepared to consider those who may not have reached the pinnacle in their chosen field but nevertheless have obtained vital business experience that, coupled with the other attributes discussed earlier, will allow them to make a very useful and competent contribution. The emphasis today has to be on director competence first and foremost. Practically everything else can be grafted on as time progresses.

Finally, it is wise not to seek directors who are already heavily committed to other boards. Some professional independent directors (those who make a full-time career of sitting on boards) claim that, by working 70 hours a week or more, they can manage 10 or more appointments. This does not work. Apart from scheduling constraints, the average board appointment today, if conscientiously pursued, consumes a minimum of 18 to 20 days per year. More demanding positions and those of board and key committee chairmen can add at least 50 percent to this figure. Five or six appointments seem to be the practical maximum that a person seeking board positions on a full-time basis can reasonably accommodate. Executives who are employed full time now often are restricted to one, at the most two, outside directorships.

Many potential directors today interview the corporation that is seeking their services. They do so to determine whether the company concerned is a desirable appointment and to allow inquiries to take place on both sides to determine if the nomination to the board is mutually desirable.

The nominating committee sometimes considers senior management appointments, particularly that of the CEO, although it is often better to strike a separate ad hoc selection committee for the latter purpose.

A final word: Some chairmen feel it is their duty, perhaps even their right, to chair the nominating committee. Such situations should be approached cautiously. Too much influence, too much concentration of power has a number of negatives, not least of which is too narrow a perspective on board recruitment and succession. The position of chairman of the nominating committee should be reserved for a senior independent board member, perhaps the vice chairman or someone with the potential to become chairman down the road. Boards tend to deal more strongly with CEO succession than with the pivotal appointment of a potential new chairman. It is time to compensate for this oversight.

Executive Committee

There is one committee for which we would urge caution in deciding to form, and this is the executive committee. The concept is quite sound: The executive committee, which usually consists of the chairman, the CEO, and three or four other senior directors, meets between board meetings to handle matters on which management may seek advice or to deal with any urgent issues that have arisen and that, as a matter of expediency, should be dealt with prior to the next scheduled board meeting. Some executive committees are delegated certain powers that enable them to take actions and decisions when they are needed quickly, eliminating the necessity of calling a full board meeting.

According to Gillies:

> The difficulty with executive committees is that they tend to lead to
> two tiers of board members. This sometimes has the unfortunate con-
> sequence of making the non-executive [committee] members too de-
> pendent on the executive committee, thereby cutting down on their
> contribution to discussions and development of policy at the board
> level. Moreover, the executive committee can become the servant of
> management, since they often work closely together on a large num-
> ber of issues.[12]

In fact, executive committees sometimes preempt both the work and the authority of the full board. Executive committees often assume authority that, in reality, they should not have. The all-important thing to remember is that all committees report to, and are accountable to, the statutory board—period. All minutes of executive committee meetings must be made available to the full board. It would be prudent to have an item on every board meeting agenda that allows for consideration and ratification of all decisions taken by the executive committee since the previous board meeting. In the extreme, the board may wish even to countermand an executive committee decision if the board deems that it is not in the best interests of the organization. The board certainly has the authority to do so; this authority cannot be removed, even by board resolution.

The practice of creating an executive committee appears to be diminishing in all but the largest corporations and some in the financial sector, where events occur quite rapidly. According to a *Boardroom* newsletter 2001 governance survey, only approximately 20 percent of companies had an executive committee. In the comparable 1999 survey, less than one-third of companies had such a committee. Be cautious in establishing an executive committee. In this age of information technology, the Internet and e-mail, teleconferencing, and so on, it is relatively simple to call meetings at short notice. The last thing one would wish for is a "board within a board."

In summary, almost any board, large or small, should have the following key committees:

- Audit
- Compensation/human resources
- Nominating
- Corporate governance

Quite a few other committees may be added, including those involved with strategic planning, corporate risk, pensions, environmental matters, and public policy. Boards sometimes assign a separate committee to strategic planning. This could be a very smart move. Otherwise, the type of company and its activities will dictate whether other committees should be struck on a permanent basis.

MAINTAINING EFFECTIVE REPORTING LINKS

Chapter 4 dealt with the actual mechanisms for holding meetings. A wider requirement exists to keep directors and the board informed. Boards and other committees can be excellent ways to spread the workload and to improve board effectiveness. But their value diminishes if directors are not kept advised of what is going on.

In one major financial institution, the conduct review committee met regularly prior to each board meeting. At the board meeting itself, the chairman of the conduct review committee gave an oral report, which was minuted in a very abbreviated form—and that was it. The minutes of the conduct review committee were not made generally available, unless asked for, which no director ever did. The life blood of the financial institution was at risk on a daily basis, loans were being approved ranging from the modest in size to the very largest offered by the bank, and directors were provided with a two-line commentary on each. This information was scarcely sufficient for the directors to claim that they, as individuals, had pursued the necessary degree of due diligence if things had gone awry.

Unfortunately, this kind of information gap seems to be prevalent in many companies and organizations today. Someone, somewhere in the organization, makes a value judgment as to what information all directors should receive; that person is not always correct. A policy regarding the dissemination of information to all directors must be established.

Obviously, oscillation between paucity of information and information overload is not useful; there has to be a balance. The chairman plays a crucial role in ensuring this balance. Many recent major corporate failures over the past 15 to 20 years show evidence of actions being taken in committee that were not properly reported to the full board. Or if the actions were reported, the reports were based on incomplete or obscure information that constrained prudent ratification of the committee's actions and decisions. One could suggest that elements of the Sunbeam and Enron fiascos fell into this category.

Boards must deal appropriately with the implications of risk to the business (as set out in Chapter 6). This means that directors must be provided with an opportunity to participate in (and/or ratify) all significant decisions involving risk, regardless of whether they have been dealt with in a committee or placed on the agenda for the full board. There is no justification for limiting the consideration of risk to bigger companies. The size of the enterprise should play no role in identification of major risks. It may be a simpler exercise for smaller companies, but, as Kevin Brown, industry editor of the London *Financial Times*, stated:

> But do reach a board consensus about the significant risks to strategic objectives in your business. And do make sure that clear decisions

have been made about how risks are monitored, and who is to do it. There needs to be clarity about which member of the board [or senior management] is to champion the design and implementation of the review process, and whether it is to be delegated to a subcommittee. If it is, think about setting up a risk committee, rather than overburdening the audit committee.[13]

Effective reporting links are essential. The quality of board decisions can only be as good as the quality of information provided to it. Managing the quantity and quality of such information is a vital component of the chairman's job. As Leighton and Thain say:

> . . . [I]n many companies, the information package sent to directors before each meeting is often too thick, takes too long to read, is difficult to understand, leaves problems buried in the numbers, and is not pointed towards relevant action options. Information is presented in raw form, leaving directors to discern the issues and meaning. It take time and trouble on the part of those responsible for the board to sift through the data, sort out irrelevant material, and digest it in meaningful form for the board to deal with; many managers take the path of least resistance and, when in doubt, throw in everything but the kitchen sink, hiding behind the defence that "it's in there—you must not have read the material carefully enough." Most directors who lack the time and commitment to sort through it all and make their own analysis remain on the outside of active decision-making and consequently often develop cynical and critical attitudes towards management.
>
> Unless understood and dealt with by the chairman, the basic problems in the form and content of the information process make it extremely difficult to control and guide the management of the company.[14]

CHAPTER 8

Board Evaluation— Assessing the Passing Grade

His promises were, as he then was, mighty;
But his performance, as he is now, nothing.

—William Shakespeare, *King Henry VIII*

THE CONCEPT OF BOARD PERFORMANCE

Up to now, there has been very little encouragement for directors to become trained in the art of direction (as opposed to management). In fact, even if directors are interested in learning the finer points of the job, limited material has been available to help them. The tendency has been to learn at the boardroom table, often by listening to others purportedly more experienced. This approach has evolved in favor of a structured approach to corporate governance including the essential need to perform in a diligent and responsible manner.

Corporate governance demands attention not only to the specific needs of the corporation but also to the many legal, political, economic, and social factors now demanded by society. These factors can include escalating pressure by shareholders for the board to "perform" as well as a need to comply to an increasing degree of regulation and involvement by statutory bodies, such as securities commissions and stock exchanges. Corporate governance also requires attention to the demands of special interest groups, often described as stakeholders, which are becoming increasingly more strident in their requests (e.g., to maintain employment at uneconomical plants).

The trend, therefore, is moving toward a system of evaluation of board performance based on its efficiency and effectiveness in meeting a broad range of objectives.

Unfortunately, certain events can occur over which the board may have little or no control. Clearly, any entrepreneurial activity at some time or other involves risk. The good board tries to assess this degree of risk and makes responsible decisions that reflect this evaluation. However, two things may happen:

1. Economic factors come into play that could not reasonably be contemplated.
2. Political decisions are made that can affect outcomes which were not previously anticipated.

Nonetheless, today it is politically expedient to make directors accountable for these events. In light of this current demanding environment, the board must be prepared to improve its ability to perform.

How does one both set objectives for the board and measure performance in relation to these objectives? How is the performance of individual directors evaluated to assess their contribution to the overall equation?

Robert Kirk Mueller has written many books on management and corporate governance. Indeed, as early as 1978 he wrote *New Directions for Directors* which contained a chapter entitled "Boardworthiness" and a comprehensive appendix entitled "Director Effectiveness."[1] It must have been somewhat of a disappointment to him that the trend to implement many of his ideas didn't catch on until the very end of his life.

Directors & Boards: A Director's Performance Appraisal was adapted from Mueller's monograph entitled *Boardworthiness*. While this and other publications are out of print, their ideas are as valid today as they have ever been.

Mueller stated perceptively:

> Elusive standards and group anonymity have long masked individual directors' contribution to company performance. But with increasing public concern [in 1993] about corporate behaviour, critics are asking, "Are directors boardworthy?"

Until recently, it would have been indelicate, at best presumptive, to suggest that boards and their members should be subject to performance appraisals. But expulsions from boardrooms, revelations of insider dealing and other unacceptable practices, plus the increased frequency of restructuring followed by lags in certain corporations' performance, have raised the issue of inadequate director effectiveness and performance. . . .

Criteria for membership on corporate boards traditionally have been elusive and purposely ambiguous. Boardworthiness is often assumed to accompany election of a director. And too few boards, board chairmen, and chief executive officers ever really tackle the question of their effectiveness. Considering the aroused public concern over corporate behaviour, the tolerance of shareholders and fellow directors to cases of dereliction of duty and pedestrian oversight in the boardroom remains surprisingly high.[2]

Often chairmen and, where the positions are combined, chief executives are understandably chary about evaluating their boards and their peers who sit on them as directors. Nevertheless, these evaluations are one of the chairman's primary responsibilities. Chairmen faced with the need to build or rebuild their boards to meet modern demands, many of which are increasingly being imposed by major shareholders and investment and financial institutions, must examine critically the effectiveness of the board as a whole as well as all it's members, including themselves. Board evaluations focus on the answer to one basic question: How well is the board doing in relation to current and future needs of the enterprise?

PERFORMING EFFECTIVELY

Any assessment of board effectiveness usually involves an examination of the board's decision making or its achievement of specific goals, such as an acquisition or diversification strategy. However, the need to maintain checks and balances on management must not be overlooked or be superficial. In so doing, the emphasis must always remain strategically based. Too often the board concentrates on reviewing history, rather than focusing on the future. Both are important, but board members can do very little about past events, other than to take steps both to prevent a recurrence of, and redress, an adverse trend. The destiny of the corporation lies in the future, and any board agenda must focus on optimizing future outcomes.

With the rise of stock exchange and shareholder activism and demonstrations of concern by lawmakers and other regulatory authorities in light of highly visible corporate failures, the performance of boards of directors has been focused on as never before. In addition, certain emotive issues, such as excessive executive compensation and mediocre corporate results, have resulted in negative public perceptions about boards.

The modern approach to corporate governance is espoused particularly in reports such as the "Blue Ribbon Report on Director Professionalism" published by the National Association of Corporate Directors in the United States; the Toronto Stock Exchange Committee's Report on Corporate Governance (the recently published Saucier report); and the Cadbury, Greenbury, and Hampel reports prepared for the London Stock Exchange, now consolidated into the Combined Code. All these reports have resulted in pressure, sometimes regulation, to ensure improved corporate governance, hence performance of boards of directors.

The Toronto Stock Exchange report, for example, does not beat about the bush in advocating as Guideline 5: "Every board of directors should implement a process to be carried out by the nominating committee or other appropriate committee for assessing the effectiveness of the board as a whole, the committees of the board and the contribution of individual directors."[3] The Toronto Stock Exchange was somewhat visionary in making its guidelines voluntary rather than mandatory insofar. Reporting issuers (the report only was implemented by the Toronto and Montreal stock exchanges) are obliged to state in their annual reports or accompanying information circulars *how* they comply or otherwise. The Hampel report in the United Kingdom followed the same approach of voluntary compliance in the hope that pressure from the public and from peers would promote high levels of conformity. However, the recent Combined Code and the Turnbull report impose compliance on all companies listed on the London Stock Exchange.

Experience has shown, in Canada at least, that larger companies tend to follow the spirit and the application of the guidelines more closely than smaller reporting issuers. Regarding Guideline 5, meaningful compliance at the overall board level has yet to exceed 50 percent. Individual director performance assessment is likely to be far lower, probably well under 20 percent.

Matthew Barrett, chairman of the Bank of Montreal, in 1994 described individual director assessment as being "an intellectually elegant concept but politically impractical."[4] He may have been correct at the time. However, since then even the Bank of Montreal has made giant steps forward in improving its approach to corporate governance. Interestingly enough, in spite of Barrett's comments, in 1995 the Bank of Montreal was one of the first major corporations to institute a sophisticated and meaningful performance assessment program, both for the board as a whole and for individual directors, using the peer review technique (a process that is very difficult to implement well).

The best way to assess board and director performance is by using carefully crafted questionnaires. Questionnaires are recommended because they are objective, and objectivity is vital in an emotionally sensitive context. To be effective, questionnaires must:

1. *Employ a methodology that is capable of self-assessment.* In other words, members of a board of directors, either collectively or individually, can work through the questionnaire and, if they are honest with themselves, derive positive and constructive output. Naturally, others who are sufficiently familiar with the activities of the board and its individual members, such as the chairman, can use the questionnaire too. However, a process capable of self-determination versus only being evaluated by others can provide an impetus and a framework within which to improve one's own performance while maintaining confidentiality over a sensitive procedure.

2. *Establish a datum.* Most board member and individual director schemes fail in their effectiveness because they do not do so. Merely asking whether board meetings are too long or too short, or whether sufficient paperwork is provided or not, is highly subjective and caters to individual opinion. Asking or assessing whether someone is technically or otherwise competent also runs the risk of subjectivity. Against what standards is one making judgment? A continuum against which to assess responses is far preferable as one is seeking to highlight strengths and weaknesses, not assess a pass or failing grade.

As one distinguished board chairman suggested, one does not need the benefit of a performance appraisal system to decide if a director is pulling his weight or not. Those skilled in human resource attributes will be able to determine this quite independently. Some means must be found to differentiate between experienced boards and novice boards. Similarly, someone newly appointed to the board should not be held to the same standard of performance as someone who has been around for some significant amount of time.

The aim of board and director performance evaluations is a determination of the means to improve. The key words of the assessment and evaluation process are competence and effectiveness.

ASSESSING HOW THE BOARD IS DOING

A continuum is a way to try to channel those completing the questionnaires into assessing where on a scale of achievement they judge the board or an individual director to be. A continuum does not seek black-or-white responses; rather, the subject is graded on a graduated scale that can be interpreted flexibly by the respondents according to their experience.

Five degrees of response are suggested:

1. *Just Developing.* This choice allows respondents who are either unfamiliar with the area being questioned or who realize some deficiency to indicate that they consider the board or themselves to be at the lower end of the spectrum.
2. *Room for Improvement.* Here respondents assess some degree of achievement or capability but suggest that there is scope for improved performance.
3. *Meets Most Criteria.* More experienced boards and many more experienced directors will likely indicate this degree of compliance. It shows a good understanding of the area under discussion but leaves a slight amount of room for further development.
4. *Optimal Performance.* Although the heading can indicate that respondents feel that they or the board are already on the top rung, it can also highlight an individual or board strength.
5. *Not Applicable.* This column should be reserved for those relatively few instances where the person completing the questionnaire genuinely feels unable to respond by virtue, for example, of being too new on the board or never having experienced the scenario posed by the question. This column must be used with extreme caution and definitely not as a way to duck a disconcerting issue.

The rationale behind the continuum approach is that truthful responses will tend to demonstrate a profile of those particular elements which questionnaire responses have shown as just developing or with room for improvement. By highlighting areas in need of improvement, it is hoped that the individual concerned or the board as a whole will direct energy toward a specific program of corporate governance development. Even more meaningful will be a further assessment in six months or a year, without reference to the previous assessment, to note if any movement has been achieved. This reassessment, in itself, should provide the potential for intrinsic personal satisfaction.

The next stage is to develop evaluative criteria based on the functions of the board. A typical abbreviated checklist can follow these lines:

- *Organizing the Board.* This can deal with the definition of the board's powers, its role and responsibilities, the distinction between direction and management, the differentiation between the powers and responsibilities of the chairman and CEO.
- *The Board as a Working Group.* Does current board makeup reflect an appropriate spectrum of expertise and experience? Does the board set and systematically review its objectives? Has the board considered its balanced self-perpetuation/succession?
- *Education and Training.* This covers the fields of induction, appreciation of board philosophy and risk criteria, mechanisms to review the quality of decision making, and identification of the board's strengths and weaknesses.
- *Selection and Appointment of the Board.* Does the board establish director job specifications? Is there a separate chairman and CEO, or if not a nominated lead director? What is the composition of key committees? Are all shareholders' interests considered impartially?
- *Meetings of the Board.* How effective are procedures surrounding preparation and holding of board meetings? Do directors demonstrate adequate briefing and attend regularly? How effectively are board meetings conducted? Do directors query concerns outside board meetings?
- *Ethics.* How about codes of corporate behavior and integrity? Is the board sensitive to a strong sense of appropriateness, and does it investigate serious concerns? Does it promote an environment of corporate social responsibility?

- *Vision, Mission, and Values.* Are the objectives of the enterprise consistent with the needs of all major stakeholders? Does the board take the initiative in directing the review of corporate and financial options? Is the implementation of all policies, plans, and obligations monitored?
- *Maintaining an Oversight.* How valid is the internal control function? Is there appropriate delegation of authority and responsibility? How effective are communications at every level?

The development of a sound board evaluation procedure is significantly more complex than this checklist illustrates. The design of performance questionnaires is quite complex and usually builds in checks to try to overcome potential subjective bias by asking similar questions in different ways. Indeed, one questionnaire used successfully by the author had 90 questions relating in detail to the topics listed.

This type of board evaluation questionnaire is not designed to judge the quality or effectiveness of the board's decision making, or the success of the company in achieving certain specified objectives. It concentrates purely on the performance of the board in the sense of how it operates. Success in decision making and the accomplishment of objectives is measured much more easily, and is usually demonstrated by financial achievement. However, because the operating behavior of companies varies so widely, dependant on a variety of conditions, it is considered far better to obtain a sense of how the board performs as an entity, and where improvement may be achieved.

The analysis of board performance questionnaires is also quite a critical procedure, as the objective is to try to identify key trends. There is never a passing grade, only some attempt to correlate where individual board members feel the board is currently on the continuum. In cases where directors have been carefully instructed how to complete board performance questionnaires, it is surprising how much consensus there is in identifying and highlighting strengths and weaknesses.

Because of the relative anonymity involved with questionnaires, respondents seem to feel relaxed enough to be critical where criticism is merited. Hence areas can be selected for attention and improvement. This is all that such a performance evaluation program attempts to do. The chairman then is responsible for collecting and sharing the results with colleagues and putting in place a specific time line to deal with areas highlighted for attention.

INDIVIDUAL DIRECTOR PERFORMANCE

In meeting the needs of the organization, directors must be able to demonstrate a deep interest and commitment to the role they are playing. They must demonstrate competence in their role as it relates to the corporation, and they must be able to participate actively in the affairs of the enterprise insofar as their equitable contribution demands. As Mueller states:

> No more can a director merely direct (if he or she ever did), or just merely reflect. Questions of whether the director is an advocate or an advisor, a tiger or a lamb, a figurehead or a keeper of a fiduciary trust, are welling up in boardrooms. We are witnessing an overdue rethinking of the philosophy, concept, structure, composition, role and effectiveness of the board and the fitness of individual directors.[5]

Mueller drew up a list of nine basic characteristics of individual directors, plus one additional for the chairman of the board, and against each of them set out a specification of behavior for each of three grades: honors, pass, and fail. The problem with this approach—which, for its day, was exceptionally perceptive—is that a director may not receive the same grade in all areas. She may merit honors for, say, 40 percent of the characteristic, a pass for 30 percent, and fail for the remaining 30 percent. What overall grade does such a director deserve?

This book advocates the tried and tested competency questionnaire approach for individual directors. In many respects, it is similar to the board questionnaire described above. It presents a list of questions covering many of the characteristics Mueller specified and seeks responses on the same continuum as provided for the board evaluation questionnaire. Through the use of this questionnaire, it becomes possible to identify strengths and weaknesses of each individual director and to seek to improve performance either by a process of self-determination or with some help from an outside resource.

This book does not suggest that an attempt be made to assess honors, passing, or failing grades; rather an attempt should be made to identify strengths and weaknesses, the latter in particular where there could be scope for improvement. Different interpretations of results should be considered based on the director's experience, basic expertise, and tenure. Higher standards should be expected of longer-serving and more experienced members of the board than of relatively recent recruits.

The following list, freely adapted from Mueller's writings, sets out categories to consider.

- *Competence as a Director.* This area attempts to cover such aspects as chemistry with other board members, peer relationships, communication skills, philosophical alignment, and well-rounded business experience.
- *Independence.* This is a crucial characteristic and deals with how a director deals with personal convictions, exercises diplomacy, avoids conflicts, expresses contrary views, and avoids caving in to pressure.
- *Preparedness.* How well is the director briefed and prepared ahead of time? Does he continually network with corporate peers and understand the concept of potential board conflicts of interest? Does he understand the statutory, fiduciary, legal liability, and governance roles? Is he well read, and does he keep abreast of relevant business trends and exercise responsibility in shaping policy?
- *The Director in Practice.* Does she demonstrate the exercise of due diligence, ask probing questions but avoid interrogation to demonstrate knowledge? Does she avoid trespassing into management's domain? Does she demonstrate a keen ability to evaluate performance, both company and individual?
- *Ambassadorship.* Is he prepared to use his influence constructively while respecting disclosure rules? Is he personable, articulate, and sophisticated in representing the company?
- *Ethics.* This area is similar to the board characteristic but is applied at the personal level; does the director demonstrate high integrity and exemplary behavior?
- *Attendance.* Does she plan ahead and schedule to attend a high proportion of board and committee meetings, or present a valid excuse? Is she available for contact and counsel by other board members and senior management outside of meetings?
- *Committee Service.* Does he understand the need and process for committees? Does he encourage staff support and input but carry an equitable portion of the workload himself?
- *Developing the Enterprise.* Is she a positive force and independent thinker? Is she knowledgeable regarding trends, strategic developments, and development opportunities? Does she seek to add personal value to the company's growth dimensions? Does she feel her membership on the board continues to be justified?

Once again, it is best not to consider these points in isolation. As with board performance questionnaires, individual director evaluations must be devised very carefully with a small but essential element of cross-verification to reduce the chance of personal bias. Additionally, skill in the analysis of such questionnaires is essential.

The question often crops up as to whether the evaluation process should be conducted by the chairman who assesses his colleagues, by the individuals individually, or by a process of peer evaluation. All three methods have been used with varying degrees of success. It is preferable that the least threatening approach be adopted on what is, according to human nature, a sensitive and sometimes challenging task. Therefore, individual assessment completion is to be preferred, in private and, if necessary anonymously, but this may not be necessary.

Again, the objective is not to generate a passing or failing grade. Neither is the procedure to be used to fire someone who is not performing satisfactorily. The trauma of an evaluation procedure generally is not required to determine that. The sole objective is to highlight those areas where directors may feel they need, or have the scope, to improve and perhaps require some help and assistance to achieve it. Indeed, results have shown remarkable consensus by many members of a board in identifying shortcomings that require much broader attention than individual director counseling.

Board chairmen often are as capable of completing assessments regarding their colleagues as other directors are about each other. Each process has its uses and has been demonstrated with relative success by some organizations. This book endorses the self-assessment system as being the most appropriate for the level of individuals concerned.

However, the chairman plays an invaluable role in counseling colleagues on the results of the individual director performance evaluation process. The chairman's interpersonal skills and empathy should be sufficiently developed that colleagues are prepared to receive constructive feedback.

THE CHAIRMAN CANNOT BE LEFT OUT

What about the performance of the chairman of the board? Chairmen must be able to be evaluated on all of the characteristics that apply to individual directors. In addition, chairmen must meet another set of challenges. While the continuum and questionnaire approach is totally relevant, chairmen have a great deal more responsibility than individual directors. Mueller's list of honors performance demonstrates just what is required of chairmen (see Exhibit 8.1).

As before, the items listed in the exhibit are by no means exhaustive, and it is strongly recommended that a separate questionnaire be designed for board chairmen.

How can chairmen make use of the findings of such a personal assessment?

First and foremost, the questionnaire is a valuable device for self-improvement. Honest responses can indicate clearly which areas have room for some improvement. Not everyone is going to achieve optimal grades—all people have some frailties and failings. However, if the chairman tends to be autocratic, for example, some outside influence will be needed to attempt to correct this.

The growth in the use of nominating and corporate governance committees has meant that the most senior board members usually have been selected to fill the majority of positions on these panels. In those cases where the positions of chairman and CEO are combined, the lead director normally is selected from among the chairman of one of these two committees. Whether a one-on-one format is preferred or a small group of wise men is selected to discuss the sensitive feedback process with the chairman is a matter of choice. Whichever format is selected, it must be conducted entirely in a positive and constructive light. As with board and individual director assessment processes, the objective is to generate improvement in effectiveness. Improvement can take place only in an environment where there is a strong impetus to perform better in the future. Subsequent questionnaire responses will demonstrate whether improvement has occurred.

DESIGNING AN APPROPRIATE PERFORMANCE EVALUATION SYSTEM

The questionnaire process with responses measured against a performance range is one of the best performance appraisal systems. However, not only does the administration of such a sensitive process need to be designed with care, but those who participate must be instructed very carefully in its completion and analysis. Many organizations have used similar appraisal systems to assess managerial performance. Bear in mind that assessment of an individual director and his or her com-

Exhibit 8.1   Chairman of the Board—Honors Grade.

- Understands and believes in significant difference of roles of chairman (as agent of the board) and chief executive officer (appointed by and responsible to the board) whether both titles are held by one person or by separate persons.

- Prepares carefully for meetings. Gives thoughtful consideration to making meetings the most effective use of time of those assembled.

- Insists on reports being properly prepared in advance and distinguishes between information and material requiring board action.

- Keeps discussions on major strategic or policy matters.

- Insists on advance review of presentations where appropriate and when needed.

- Is competent in chairing and managing group dynamics and thoughtful in agenda management.

- Considers what executive officers need to focus on at meetings and coaches them on director education and perceptions.

- Properly balances exposure of board to advocate and adversary views on major issues.

- Encourages constructive debate and independent viewpoints. Endeavours to make each meeting an interesting and rewarding experience for each participant.

- Effective leader with personal respect and established collateral with each member.

- Sees that candidates are developed for chairman and CEO succession, whether both titles are held by one person or separate persons.

- This involves an education and testing process plus understanding of different qualifications for chairmanship and chief executive officer roles.

Source: Adapted from Robert Mueller, *Boardworthiness* (Presidents Association of the American Management Association), p. 19.

petence and effectiveness in a position is different from an assessment of managerial traits and performance per se.

Careful introduction of the performance appraisal system is essential. A knowledgeable and independent facilitator is recommended who can introduce the subject in two stages:

1. Overall familiarity with the instrument
2. Follow-up training in its application

Respondents can gain overall appreciation of the instrument in a group of five or six participants. (Too large a group can reduce the effectiveness of a presentation.) This appreciation session, possibly using visual aids, can demonstrate that the instrument is classified as "incremental" rather than "definitive." The point is to convey the message that the first task is to try to identify strengths and weaknesses on a *relative* basis. If the appraisal system allows a board to define a strength as it's monitoring role and, at the same time, identify scope for improvement in its strategic role, this will be an indication of its effectiveness. No attempt is made to quantify *how much* improvement is needed, merely that improvement could be beneficial.

A follow-up training session is recommended to familiarize participants with the process. This session is best conducted one on one. Here the facilitator presents a dummy exercise, with examples, but with no direct relevance to the individual or the board in question. The session is important because people tend to feel most comfortable with mediocrity. In other words, without training, many people tend to place their responses toward the middle of the scale. To do this loses much of the impact. The whole idea of the system is to highlight strengths and weaknesses, so that there is a positive force to seek improvement where advantageous.

The key is to emphasize the questionnaire's nonthreatening aspect. Unless the board as a whole wishes it, appraisals are kept anonymous. If a summary of the board appraisal is required, then either the independent facilitator creates the summary in conditions of strict confidentiality or the respondents' identities are removed from the forms. Much of the benefit of the personal assessments is derived by the individual realizing where he or she can improve performance. However, many boards may consider that an independent facilitator can be useful in discussing, again on a one-to-one basis, areas that have been highlighted and then preparing an anonymous summary for the chairman and/or the board as a whole. This involvement of someone independent may highlight, as an example, a need for the board to consider a different approach to board orientation or succession planning, both important elements of board activity in their own right.

Thus far, the method and application of questionnaire administration has been discussed. The next stage is implementation. At least initially, rarely should implementation occur in-house. Major difficulties encountered are usually those involving personalities and sensitivities. Equally fundamental is the expertise necessary for implementation and, most important of all, the perceived independence of the individual involved.

While some would suggest that this role is best played by someone with a human resources background—after all, empathy and skill in dealing with people, particularly top-level directors and board chairmen, is a must—even more important is a thorough understanding of how a board of directors should operate and of the latest thinking and pressures to perform effectively. Therefore, a facilitator with actual board experience is preferable.

USING OR ABUSING THE PROCESS?

When completing a performance assessment, whether for a board as a whole or for an individual director, it is important to resist the temptation to assume that a lower rating on the continuum implies criticism. If the person completing the questionnaire feels that there is insufficient rotation of board and committee members, then this area should be marked as having "room for improvement." If the respondent feels that there is virtually no rotation and the board is at risk of becoming stale, then a "just developing" response could indicate, indeed emphasize, one area where the board should try to improve.

Not all questions are likely to carry equal weight. Obviously, some topics will be more important than others. The process is not trying to differentiate. What is sought is not only an element of consensus around the board table but areas in which effectiveness can be improved. If, in the extreme, the consensus is that everything is optimal and there is a lack of desire to embrace the performance evaluation process, there would seem to be little point in wasting directors' time in going through the motions of the exercise.

Some questions undoubtedly will require soul searching. It needs a brave person to mark him- or herself toward the lower end of the spectrum in answering: "Fits in well with the needs of the corporation." Similarly, some directors may hesitate before responding to: "Would resign rather than be considered captive." It takes a fair degree of tough-mindedness and objectivity to give honest responses. If factors such as these had been highlighted ahead of time for the boards of some of the more spectacular corporate failures, those failures might have been avoided.

While possessing one vote, the chairman of the board is also the leader or the helmsman of the enterprise. Any additional questions posed regarding the performance of this individual are solely in regard to the individual's board position. If that person happens to hold the CEO's baton as well, his or her performance in that role must be evaluated separately according to quite different performance criteria.

Finally, those completing the questionnaires may feel uncomfortable in relating some of the questions to their specific experiences. The questions may not be truly applicable, or directors may feel they are too new in the position to answer in a meaningful manner. In such circumstances, it is perfectly acceptable to answer "not applicable." One should attempt to use this response category sparingly.

CHAPTER 9

The Supercharged Board

A victory is twice itself when the achiever brings home full numbers.

—William Shakespeare, *Much Ado About Nothing*

STRATEGIC PRINCIPLES

Ask many directors what they think is their principal task as a board member and they often suggest that it is to ride herd on management and to oversee statutory legal compliance. By doing so, they feel they will have acquitted themselves with distinction and limited their personal legal liability exposure.

Sir Ronnie Hampel's committee in the United Kingdom, which reviewed the initial Cadbury report and the subsequent code initiated by the London Stock Exchange, may have said it best when it stated that "[T]he importance of corporate governance lies in its contribution both to business prosperity and accountability. In the United Kingdom, the latter has pre-occupied much public debate over the past few years. We now wish to see the balance corrected."[1] To correct the imbalance, the Hampel committee suggested that better rather than more disclosure should be expected regarding the internal dealings of British boardrooms. Instead of merely complying with a code of conduct, [listed] companies would be expected to include a narrative about how broad principles have been applied. (Interestingly, this is precisely the same conclusion that the recent Saucier report came to.)

As discussed, Canada's own Toronto Stock Exchange report established 14 "voluntary" guidelines. By not insisting on strict compliance but by imposing the requirement for a narrative explaining how and why companies either complied or did not, chairman Peter Dey hoped that peer pressure and public opinion could persuade companies to improve their standards of corporate governance. The approach has been modestly successful for larger listed companies. Smaller companies have had lower degrees of compliance, but compliance is improving over time. However, surveys consistently show that the business community has overwhelmingly welcomed the guidelines and feel that they have helped to improve the quality of corporate governance, even if individual company compliance is sometimes variable and, in some instances, a little problematical.

While directed toward listed companies, these recommendations cover both the broader business prosperity and accountability aspects suggested by Hampel. It sometimes has been suggested, perhaps simplistically, that a board of directors is responsible for just two things: maintaining an oversight and checks and balances on management; but much more important, ensuring the future viability and prosperity of the enterprise. And as been suggested, directors are sometimes delinquent in their attention to the latter.

Many directors, some of whom are distinguished public figures, do not feel directors should become involved with the strategic planning *process*. Even the distinguished Canadian academic Henry Mintzberg suggests that boards sometimes overplan and underthink! Mintzberg suggests that "strategic planning" is, in fact, an oxymoron, similar to "military intelligence." In *The Rise and Fall of Strategic Planning*, Mintzberg states that: "Strategy making is the critical thinking required of leadership and evolves from individual visions and creativity, whereas planning is a helpful analytic and formal process that organizes, communicates, and develops action elements throughout the enterprise for the implementation of strategic thinking." He succinctly observes that "the work of creating strategy cannot be programmed like that of shovelling coal."[2]

Nevertheless, the board does have a definite responsibility to:

- Ensure that the enterprise devotes time and resources in order to focus on the future

- Ensure that management prepares and implements specific strategic operational goals

The board has a specific role to play when researching and examining the threats and opportunities surrounding and relevant to the enterprise, and when deciding long-term objectives, by virtue of its broader perspectives on the business. After all, to obtain the benefit of this breadth of expertise is one of the principal reasons why companies seek outside independent directors. But management has to assume a more enveloping responsibility when the mechanistic stages of evaluating strategy and ultimately implementation are reached.

BRINGING DIRECTORS UP TO SPEED

Recent surveys indicate that many companies now have director orientation programs. However, it is likely that the majority of medium-size and small enterprises do not. Volunteer organizations are even less likely to have such programs despite the fact that, with their more regular turnover of directors, they have an even more pressing need to ensure continuity and maintenance of the organization's mission, vision, and values.

Director orientation is the process of bringing new directors up to speed, efficiently and effectively. Some board manuals set out procedures and policies toward expenses and the like and also include financial statements and a reproduction of mission, vision, and values. But the manuals are not likely to contain as much material describing the philosophy of the organization, its principal stakeholders, its current and most important challenges and threats, and so on.

Experienced directors of major corporations usually decry the need for orientation, saying "All our directors are experienced business people, they don't need educating." Yet other directors often say things like "It took me at least a year before I really found my way around the board, who were the movers and shakers, and really gained an insight into where the company was going. During that time, I was expected to pull my weight in fighting fires about which I knew practically nothing."

Ideally, therefore, board newcomers must receive adequate and meaningful briefing materials. Complicated financial statements containing a mass of historical figures, which accountants can understand but the average board member may not, are rarely useful. New directors need a fairly simple guide as to whether things are good or bad, above or below average; whether there are avoidable or unavoidable variances from the planned outcome; and what the effect on the bottom line is likely to be. A lot of effort should be spent in devising and presenting information in the form of meaningful indices and ratios that can explain quite simply how the organization is doing.

Budgets are another area of vulnerability. Obviously, a budget goal of selling 1000 units in a year and only having sold 300 after nine months tells a vital story. But one multimillion-dollar enterprise insisted on maintaining such a budget even after it became completely meaningless. Budgets represent statements of intention and a datum from which to control. But they only represent best estimates at the time they were prepared. Although budgets should not be changed without sound reason, for otherwise that datum for control is lost, by the same token, controlling an enterprise on meaningless expectations is even more dangerous. Therefore, part of the mechanism for identifying risks and maintaining the integrity of internal control systems must be to ensure that explicit but realistic budgets are, and remain, in place and that progress is faithfully and regularly monitored against them.

FAMILY FIRMS

The record of family firm survival through to the second and third generations is discouraging—something on the order of 30 percent and 13 percent respectively. Sometimes the reason that it no longer exists as a family firm is an excellent one. For example, the firm may have done so well that it has achieved public status through a stock exchange listing. However, in such instances, often the family retains a majority stake and certainly relies heavily on its entrepreneurial talent to maintain the firm's profitability.

Survival in the longer term seems to devolve around how well the firm's founders have built the business, grown a management team, and ensured that it will continue to flourish relatively independently of the original family members. Entrepreneurial talent must be tied to competent management, particularly when the span of control expands beyond the effectiveness of key individuals. At this stage, family businesses need to be able to draw on the best outside advice to complement the strengths and expertise that historically have been provided by the family.

Unfortunately, family business owners, as a category, tend to hang on too long before they realize their fallibility and/or lack of immortality. Furthermore, if family members have differing views on the future of the business, the stage may be set for dissent and dispute. Fortunately, there is growing recognition of the problems family businesses encounter, and many excellent books have been published on the subject. The various approaches are too detailed to be listed here. Suffice it to state that it is essential to define family roles and have in place mechanisms for resolving any disputes that may arise.

It is also essential to involve outsiders at appropriate times that usually are earlier than the family is, psychologically, prepared to consider. In this context outsiders can mean the recruitment of additional but non-family management expertise to complement family skills. Alternatively, sometimes outsiders can contribute in a mentoring or professional consultancy capacity. (This kind of assistance tends to be for the shorter term.) Or a board of directors can be formed; in the context of the family business, the board often acts primarily in an advisory, but often essential counseling, capacity.

If an advisory board is formed, family business owners must be prepared to listen to it and act on its recommendations. Failure to do so not only discourages the recruitment of qualified persons but defeats the whole objective of seeking outside advice. The family also must disclose information, formerly held fairly closely, to these new outside advisors. This sharing of confidential information is part of the price to be paid to gain the benefits of independent advice.

A senior family member, either the patriarch or the senior sibling, almost invariably chairs the board of a family firm. Very rarely family firms, certainly those of the first generation, feel comfortable in inviting an independent outsider to assume the role. If the chairman is one of the company's major shareholders, he or she must be committed to making the concept of using outside advice work. Shareholder and operational issues must be separated, and the board must perform in an efficient and pragmatic manner. Indeed, despite the fact that the business is family-owned (and in this respect can be considered similar to a wholly owned subsidiary of any major corporation), the meeting process—preparation of the agenda, the recording of minutes, the diligent presentation of reports and proposals for key decisions—must proceed as for any other successful for-profit organization.

As mentioned, the fact that only about 30 percent of family businesses survive until the second generation is not all negative. Many companies that began based on individual entrepreneurial talent develop into highly successful listed companies and continue to thrive. But according to Patrick Caragata in *Business Early Warning Systems*:

> Depending on the industry, up to one third of new companies fail within three years. Those companies that get past this early survival hurdle may have a relatively short life. Most companies do not survive longer than 10 to 12 years. Further, the most successful companies do not have a life span longer than 40 to 50 years. Thus it is clear that the life span of companies is much shorter than the average human life span. Very simply, the life-survival skills of individuals are superior to those of companies.[3]

While Caragata's comments are a generalization, nevertheless they are very sobering. Family businesses that are able to transition successfully to become listed companies or to pass the baton to the second and even later generations are probably ahead of the curve. Initiating and implementing the changes required to succeed in future generations requires a fair amount of courage and determination.

Four excellent booklets on the subject of family firms have been published by the UK Institute of Directors in collaboration with the Stoy Centre for Family Business.[4] They are succinct, very much to the point, and emphasize communication and motivation. They attack head-on the problem of relinquishing control.

PREVENTING AND DETECTING PROBLEMS

The director's two primary tasks are focusing on the future and the continued viability and prosperity of the enterprise; and monitoring operational performance. However, it is unreasonable to expect outside directors to have either the time or necessarily the expertise to know and understand everything that is happening on a day-to-day basis. To compensate for this, directors have to develop finely tuned antennae that will indicate when problems are likely to occur and how to deal with them. Fortunately, a number of indicators are available to assist directors in this task.

The first group of indicators consists of precautionary procedures, chief of which is a sound system of budgetary control. This, in turn, implies two things: that there is a budget; and that there are means in place in order to monitor performance against this budget. Another important element is timeliness. No control mechanism is worth a dime unless it can be brought into play in time for it to be useful and effective.

There was an instance where a company suspected that one of its divisions was not performing satisfactorily and was providing incomplete reports. At the end of the second month, when suspicions were confirmed, someone was sent down from the head office to investigate. The inspector confirmed that something serious was occurring and recommended action. By the time the board considered this a third month had elapsed. It was nearly four months before the situation began to be corrected.

Prompt reports are vital in assessing a company's health. However, managers, particularly those involved in financial matters, often complain that measuring and reconciling month-end performance takes several days, even weeks. Rarely do these reports surface before the third week of the following month, meaning that, on average, much of the information is history: about four and a half to five weeks old. Managers have to understand that extreme accuracy of reporting is not always necessary. Adjustments can always be made. Consistency, one month to the next, is even more important.

In other words, a report that is, say, 80 percent factual and 20 percent estimate is fine *provided* that, on a month-over-month basis, this pattern of reporting is repeated. Gradually, over time, any inaccuracies can be adjusted and the process will become increasingly reliable. But the company has benefited by receiving early reports within days of the end of the reporting period.

Other indicators may point to problems that may exist within the organization. These indicators may be divided into three areas:

1. Communications between management and the board
2. Lack of operational procedures and/or controls inside the company
3. More wide-ranging troubles with other parties

The first group of problems that can give cause for concern often arise from structural defects in top management, such as an unbalanced management team or too much power invested in one individual. Other concerns may become evident in regard to delays in implementing board decisions, weak reporting or plain lack of sufficient records, and misguided loyalties in concealing errors and incompetence. Finally, care should be taken to avoid developing too close personal relationships, which may allow emotional criteria to intrude into the decision-making process.

Information asymmetry exists in that the board, and individual directors, can never know as much as management about the affairs of the enterprise. Hence it is equally impracticable to suggest that directors should find out everything for themselves. They must be absolutely sure to exercise due diligence, true, but they must also rely on management to a significant extent. Directors will never have enough time to inquire into every continency. The collapse of Enron Corporation in the United States is a prime example of the type of occurrence where directors most likely were either uninformed or misinformed. Therefore, a responsible balance must be sought.

Many experienced businesspeople develop a sixth sense, an intuition, that allows them to focus on potential problems. Directors without this business experience, particularly of adverse situations, will be at a disadvantage in searching for the truth or, conversely, in satisfying themselves that everything is in order.

When information, or lack of it, suggests that something is wrong, directors might ask:

- Is a budgetary control procedure in place that allows ready comparisons of actual performance against what was planned? Does this procedure cover really important criteria, such as work in process, inventories, sales, direct and variable expenses, and the like? Equally important, is the budget still valid and realistic, or have events conspired to make it meaningless? Is undue emphasis being placed on "futures": events that may or may not come to pass but are being heavily weighted as likely to happen? If so, are the estimates of probability realistic?
- How secure are the company's assets, including intellectual property (an increasingly valuable resource)? Is insurance coverage realistic, and have there been any major claims made against it? Has insurance ever been refused or coverage restricted?
- What about customer relations? The new buzz phrase, "customer relationship management," seems to have enhanced the

importance of analyzing and managing every aspect of customer relations to ensure maximum benefits to all concerned. Have there been any major complaints or concerns expressed about product quality or deliveries—or lack of them?

- Is the "grapevine" alive and well in terms of relationships with staff, at every level in the organization? What about staff turnover? Are exit interviews conducted as a matter of course, and are the results tabulated to determine reasons and trends, bearing in mind that staff retention is much less costly than recruitment and training?

- Have any statutory authorities recently conducted an unusual audit? Are any checks and balances in place to ensure that taxes and withholdings are remitted regularly and on time? Have the company's own auditors ever expressed concerns and are direct communication channels to the board available to them? Are any "creative" accounting mechanisms being used? With the increased emphasis on the role of the audit committee, communications with outside auditors much be closely monitored.

- Finally, is the company's share price monitored regularly to detect any unusual movement or fluctuations? Does anything suggest that one or more parties may be accumulating stock in anticipation of a bid or an attempt to "short" the stock? With the increased emphasis on disclosure, does the board monitor closely what is revealed to the public at large to ensure that it is truthful and timely, and that it reflects the most appropriate information at the time it was released? If circumstances have changed materially, is the company complying with the requirements for making additional disclosures?

The director's role is to question, sometimes to persist in questioning, and to obtain reasonable satisfaction. If the director does not do so, then at some stage or other, trouble may be reasonably anticipated.

In a monograph prepared for the National Association of Corporate Directors, Dr. Howard M. Schilit listed seven financial "shenanigans," which he described as actions or omissions intended to hide or distort the real financial performance or financial condition of a business entity. "They range from minor deceptions (such as failing to segregate operating from non-operating gains or losses in a clear manner) to more serious misapplications of accounting principles." Schilit lists the seven "shenanigans:"

1. Recording revenue too soon, either before the earnings process has been completed or before an exchange has occurred.
2. Recording bogus revenue, which can occur when a company receives cash or other assets in on-sales transactions but still records sales revenues. One company was charged with classifying as income one-time vendor credits that it had not actually collected.
3. Boosting income with one-time gains. Techniques using this device include recording the sale of appreciated assets at higher-than-book value, boosting profits by retiring debt, failing to segregate unusual or nonrecurring gains or losses from recurring income, burying losses under noncontinuing operations, and using a related entity to boost profits artificially.
4. Shifting expenses to a later reporting period. This can be achieved by improperly capitalizing costs as inventory or other type of asset, depreciating or amortizing costs too slowly, or failing to write off worthless assets.
5. Failing to record or disclose all liabilities. Many businesses receive cash before they have actually earned it. Such businesses are required to defer the recognition of revenue until they have discharged any attendant liability.
6. Shifting current income to a later reporting period. To achieve this, a company creates reserves by shifting sales revenue to a later period. Doing this allows the company to create a hedge against a potential future market downturn and reduce near-term profits, which is not an acceptable practice.
7. Shifting future expenses to the current period. One scenario could be that if a company has already met its income projections for the period, it may attempt to shift next year's expenses into the current period. Obviously the tax man is not very keen to allow this to happen.[5]

Many danger signals are available to alert directors. As outside board members are not intimately involved in day-to-day activities, they must know where to look and where to probe. They also must not be afraid to ask penetrating questions and seek substantiation where doubt may exist. These rights, properly asserted, need not be construed as mistrust in management. By the same token, management should be only too aware that the board of directors expects accurate, meaningful, and appropriate information.

ASSUMPTION OF RISK

It has sometimes been suggested that the majority of successful companies, at some stage in their growth and development, were faced with a decision that, if things had gone against them, could possibly have caused them to collapse, or very nearly so. This, in simple terms, is what risk is all about.

Some entrepreneurs are extremely good at evaluating risk intuitively, knowing when to take a chance, and usually pulling it off. James Doolittle was ordered grounded during World War II when he became a general, in the belief that his continuing to fly presented unnecessary risks. Doolittle is reported to have sometimes ignored the order, stating that all his risks were calculated and, therefore, little was left to chance.

If only life were that simple! Those who work in the construction industry talk about factors of safety where they calculate loads and stresses well in excess of what the structure is designed to take. Those who design aircraft know that at the moment of takeoff, the margin of safety is very slim—everything is working full out, and if, for example, an engine fails at this critical juncture, the result would more than likely be catastrophic.

In business today, decision making need not be that uncertain. The advent of sophisticated computer systems has allowed the introduction of various management tools, and critical factors can be more easily identified.

But even before computer programs were developed, various management tools existed. The first of these is well known and described variously as Pareto's law or the 80:20 rule. Pareto, an Italian economist who lived from 1848 to 1923, discovered that in most situations, the identification of the "significant few" would have a disproportionate effect on the outcome as a whole. Put another way, 20 percent of the customers could represent 80 percent of the sales volume, or 20 percent of the inventory could represent 80 percent of its value.

It is of little importance whether the precise curve of distribution follows the 80:20 rule or 75:25 or whatever. What is important is the identification of that significant few. Many years ago, a consulting company was asked by the government to identify the employment patterns for the port of Liverpool in the United Kingdom. There were, at that time, about 105,000 dockworkers and 65 employers. Because of impending threat of major industrial action, the consulting firm was allowed exactly one week to find the information required. A daunting task! However, applying Pareto's principle, the firm found that just five employers were responsible for over 70,000 jobs. Interviewing these five key firms provided information reliable enough for the report to be completed within the time allowed.

What is the lesson here for the boardroom? Applying Pareto's principle judiciously allows directors to seek key information on which to verify essential data. This in turn will allow them to make decisions based on representative facts.

Another management tool consists of stochastic decision trees. Investment decisions are almost invariably characterized by three facts:

1. Large sums of money can be involved
2. Such decisions can have long-lasting effects
3. A high degree of risk and/or uncertainty can exist

Two questions exist:

1. How to handle decisions made in conditions of uncertainty
2. How to treat separate but related investment decisions that have to be made at different points in time

The use of stochastic decision trees is outside the scope of this book. Techniques are readily available that will assist directors in quantifying the risks and probabilities attached to certain courses of action. Board members should expect management to provide this type of analysis to them.

A third management tool that is of great benefit to the board is sensitivity analysis, a technique used to identify which components of a decision are most vulnerable to change and which are not. In many situations, estimates must be made of various events in the future, such as:

- Costs
- Sales volume
- Taxation
- Timing of events

Sensitivity analysis calculates the effect of a change in these parameters. What happens if sales fall to 80 percent of projected levels, or the new plant comes on stream three months late?

This analysis allows management, and the board, to concentrate on those items that are the most sensitive to change and relegate those that are not to relative orders of magnitude without the need for precise calculation. In most studies that use this technique, sales volume and the level of variable costs are commonly more sensitive than the majority of other factors.

Surveys have established that relatively few companies employ the techniques just described to evaluate risk.

HOW ARE WE DOING AS A BOARD?

This section steps back and takes a look at how the board is doing. It may seem strange, but boards run the whole spectrum from being compact, focused, and effective to being unwieldy, rambling, and extremely frustrating. There is little point in making an issue of this because in the end we are dealing with people. People sometimes are thrown together in an environment that generates positive chemistry, and sometimes they find it extremely difficult to get along with each other. And very often those same people would interact and relate totally differently in a different work environment.

To be effective, a board of directors must be compatible. The members must enjoy working with each other. Their strengths must complement each other's. In other words, they must create synergy. The chemistry must be right. Occasionally, a very fine chamber orchestra seems to perform exquisitely without a conductor, until one realizes that the concertmaster is very subtly maintaining close control over both timing and tempo. Without an effective captain of the ship or the chairman of the board, much energy will likely be dissipated to little avail.

However, the chairman is but first among equals. He can only provide leadership. The corporate power must stem from the collective strengths of the relatively few individual directors working as a team. The modern tendency is to reduce the size of the board to a compact number, usually around 10 to 12. Some organizations believe that an even smaller number, as few as seven, is sufficient. Such a reductions causes some concern as today directors' duties are quite onerous. If committee responsibilities are added to board functions, the load on individuals may become quite large.

It is important to remember that the board is used primarily for decision making and not for incessant consideration of historical reports, witch hunting, recriminations, or other counterproductive activities. Boards must, above all, be proactive, not reactive. Their monitoring role is essential but almost a given. The board's strategic perceptions are more important, as without some vision, the enterprise could well wither and die.

Interestingly, however, most corporate failures, apart from those involving fraud or other potentially criminal acts, seem to stem from strong personalities having a disproportionate influence on their colleagues. The era of rubber-stamping is not quite dead, unfortunately. This is why the chairman must maintain a strong sense of direction without imposing her will. The chief executive officer, on the other hand, often must demonstrate leadership from the front; this is another reason why often it is not beneficial to have the CEO serve as board chairman.

The best boards operate by consensus. But consensus is not, must not be, automatic. A lot of careful preparatory work is involved. A pile of board papers should not be waiting at directors' places when they arrive for a board meeting. By the same token, decision making must be informed, not seat-of-the-pants, participation. Directors must be briefed, and well briefed. Individuals who cannot spare the time to do justice to their need to prepare should not be appointed to the board. As Tom Kierans, chairman of Petro Canada and a director of many other companies, stated:

> The days of golf in the afternoon are pretty rapidly disappearing. Dinners have become working dinners, not social events. This is all working to provide us with better boards. However, despite these improvements, there are still a substantial number of challenges to attend to. The first of these is time. We are not talking about two and a half hour board meetings and then a nice lunch. The period required before any meeting to absorb and process information, comprehend it and reflect upon it so that appropriate judgment can be exercised, is very time consuming. . . . If you add the time spent in reading and digesting board and committee minutes, preparing for meetings, actually attending regular board and committee meetings, we arrive at a substantial commitment in terms of time. It is no longer a question of throwing the stuff into your briefcase, climbing on the plane, reading it for an hour and a half, arriving at your destination, pretending that you know what everyone is talking about and re-

turning home. Board participation has become much more of an interactive process.[6]

A major problem is that many boards believe that they are above criticism—that if they make a mistake, it is largely due to causes beyond their control. This is patently not true. The majority of high-profile corporate failures in recent years can be laid at the door of unfortunate board decisions, or lack of the correct ones.

ADVISORY BOARDS

Unlike statutory boards, advisory boards can avoid potential legal liability exposure and many of the responsibilities of the statutory boards. Advisory boards appear to be coming back into fashion in a number of fairly novel ways. If advisory boards are devised to have no legal power of oversight or ability to replace management, their effectiveness lies solely in their ability to counsel and advise. Robert Mueller has listed seven likely reasons for using an advisory board:

1. A gap-filling function when the owners or owner-representatives lack time or expertise to cope with the difficulties of governing or managing an organization in a dynamic environment.
2. A resource to top management and the statutory board. The advisors supplement the expertise of the internal staff. They avoid the consequences of group-think, concinnity, and lack of objectivity when the advocates of a decision are involved in its justification or are beneficiaries of the action.
3. Providing special peer-acceptable insight in the grey area of entrepreneurship, innovation and professional business administration.
4. As an adjunct to the corporation's intelligence-gathering system for the purposes of activity or societal scans on an international or specific functional or strategic area of interest (technology, economics, marketing).
5. To identify and evaluate alternative course of action not foreseen by management or the main board.
6. To assist the CEO in resolving or reconciling serious internal differences or opinion by an objective outside judgment.
7. To provide introductions to potential customers, suppliers, or clients; develop business, government and trade relations; keep abreast of political, social and technical developments in industry, government, or universities.[7]

These are gigantic tasks in themselves and of inestimable value to the company. It is little wonder that many of the world's largest and most profitable organizations employ advisory boards, particularly in operating their overseas subsidiaries.

One of the more recent developments has been the increased use of advisory boards in the high-technology sector. It is difficult for emerging companies, with products in the developmental stage, with little cash flow but significant future potential, to attract high-caliber directors to sit on their statutory board. However, the advisory status without the concomitant liability is an attractive alternative.

Companies that elect to utilize advisory boards must be willing to use the outside talent. In other words, an advisory board is of little benefit if its advice is ignored or diluted. But such boards do provide small and medium-size companies ways to enlist expert advice at comparatively low cost.

Where does this leave the statutory board? Basically, there are two ways to use the advisory board process:

1. Retain the statutory board but bring in additional expertise, sometimes to cover specific contingencies or situations. Advisory boards also can work in those cases where recruiting top talent on a statutory basis would prove difficult or impossible.
2. Maintain the statutory board at the smallest practical level, say two or three members, purely to fulfill the legally required functions, and institute the advisory board concept for practically everything else. Family-owned businesses and start-up companies often do this.

What are the principal challenges facing chairmen of advisory boards? Often the chairman will be the same person who chairs the statutory board. This could be desirable from a communications and continuity perspective. However, the advisory board's agenda will be almost entirely strategically based. Therefore, the chairman has to concentrate energies in channeling the board's initiatives to helping the *company* make specific decisions, without necessarily endorsing a particular or, indeed, necessarily the wisest course of action. Advisory boards often provide comparative advice. The skill sets available and the very circumstance of the advisory boards' existence are not necessarily designed to provide specific business decisions.

Alternatively, advisory boards may brainstorm and identify possible courses of action, and indeed comment constructively, but, again, not necessarily recommend which course should be pursued. These boards may try to relieve management of some pressures caused by rapid growth or financial constraints. In such cases, advisory boards serve as counselors or sounding boards, which management may appreciate in times of high stress.

Another role is one of impartiality and objectivity. Advisory boards should have no ax to grind, no vested interests. Therefore, their advice can help to resolve or reconcile differences or help overcome particular challenges in a dispassionate manner. All in all, advisory boards can provide specialist counsel in a wide variety of circumstances. The chairman of such a body should take every opportunity to use its talents in the most constructive manner.

THE BOARD'S ROLE IN INNOVATION

One of the most important functions of any type of board is to ensure the future of the enterprise. A future cannot be ensured without a constant pressure to innovate. Innovation need not necessarily involve searching for new products or new technology, although this search must continue. It can relate to expanding the existing business. It can relate to joint venture opportunities or new markets. However, the board always must remain aware of the threat of competition. At the same time, it must be prepared to take advantage of opportunities that may present themselves.

The buzz word "synergy" may be a little played out, but its implications remain valid. Synergy amounts to trying to devise something for the business that, when added to something that the company already has, makes the sum greater than the component parts. This is what innovation is all about.

Innovation and change are not options. There is no such thing as a company standing still. "When you stop learning, you will soon neglect what you already know." The whole purpose of a company operating in a free enterprise environment is to take and manage risk. Without risk, it will prove difficult to innovate. Without innovation, what are the options for growth and long-term sustainability?

The innovative capacity of a company is constrained by the quality of its leadership. Most companies merit a failing grade when it comes to handling the process of continuous learning and growth. The Conference Board of Canada devised a 20-point *Corporate Innovation Checklist*, reprinted as Exhibit 9.1. Respondents were asked to complete the

Exhibit 9.1 Innovation Checklist.

- Change is a constant in our organization.
- Any of our employees will say yes to the statement: "We are an organization marked by continuous learning and growth."
- Our vision-driven organization develops processes that are aligned to and driven by that vision.
- Our organization strategically aligns its resources into innovative approaches, cutting through and across business units.
- A focus on innovation plays a major role in our corporate planning cycle.
- Time is set aside in board meetings to discuss new business and initiatives.
- New business discussions are placed first on our board agenda.
- We have a healthy balance between staff turnover and long-term employees.
- Our employees are accomplishing personal and career goals.
- This organization includes all of its stakeholders in fostering idea organization and development.
- Increase in shareholder value is constant and sustainable.
- Time to reflect on successes, failures, innovations and new ideas is included in board agendas.
- Innovation at our organization is not reactive but rather is driven by the desire to meet both internal and external need.
- Research and Development (R&D) is ingrained organization wide—it is not relegated to the back room.
- Our organization is fluid, networked, has partners and is decentralized.
- Our organization has leadership that is effective in taking innovation from an idea to a commercially viable product.
- In our organization, R&D is seen as an investment opportunity.
- Our organization has a steady stream of new products and services.
- Project teams from across the organization bring ideas from concept to customer.
- Our board accepts leadership in strategic risk management.

Source: Debra Brown, *20 Point Corporate Innovation Check List for Boards* (Conference Board of Canada, January 2001). Used with permission.

questionnaire using a scale from zero (worst) to five (best). The average score from the Conference Board's fairly broad sample was well under 50 percent.

A *Business Week* article reported that Motorola had historically been preoccupied with renewal. The company began operations in 1928, manufacturing storage batteries for home radios. Two years later it introduced radios for cars, linking radio with motion:

> Renewal had already become a driving thrust. Renewal—a change in the Company's product focus or management emphasis—has continued to be an ongoing key to Motorola's success . . . renewal—a determination to focus differently, a willingness to shed. Currently, the Company has programs under way which will allow people to communicate, through satellites to the most remote corners of the earth.[8]

How prophetic! And how true. And how far Motorola has come since 1928. Robert Mueller has written:

> Innovation is like love, humour or sex. Innovation, broadly, is useful change, and it differs from creativity or invention, in that it must be adapted to be an innovation. It can suffer from over-analysis, over-organization, and over-control. Innovation is a uniquely human quality. Therefore, a strategic plan that does not address cultural conditions within the corporation that are required to foster innovation does not qualify for my transitional model strategy.[9]

David A. H. Brown has spoken about innovation as a culture. He presented five steps for the board to undertake in implementing a process for continuous learning and growth:

1. Use strategic plans to inspire and broaden views.
2. Instill a learning culture.
3. Prepare for and profit from change and uncertainty
4. Review performance measures and management reports for progress against targets and benchmarks.
5. Review the corporate mission from time to time.

> A board should focus on solutions and initiatives. It should lead by standing behind well-planned innovation with corporate resources: people, time, money, influence and capital expenditure.[10]

CHAPTER 10

A Question of Ethics

It is preoccupation with possession, more than anything else, that prevents men living freely and nobly.

—Bertrand Russell, *Quotes for Everyday Inspiration*, CCH Canadian

CREATING AN ETHICAL FRAMEWORK

This chapter on business ethics has been included for a number of reasons. Primarily, history has shown that if the free enterprise sector does not behave responsibly, then government will intervene. Is it desirable for companies to regulate themselves or to have someone else do it?

Peter Drucker is alleged to have said that "ethics stay in the preface of the average business science book." The inference is that no one pays too much attention to how business is conducted, but that one knows that one should. In the book *Mayflower Madam*, Stanley Biddle Barrows said, "I ran the wrong kind of business, but I did it with integrity." Somewhere between these two extremes lies a balance of appropriate behavior. Currently ethics has become an important issue.

The topic of ethics assumes almost disproportionate importance when there is a high-profile instance of misbehavior. Consider when, for example, Robert Maxwell drowned, and it was found that $1.5 billion was missing from his employees' pension fund; or when the thrift company scandal hit in the United States; or when the top executives of Guinness in the United Kingdom were found to have manipulated its stock price in a hotly contested takeover battle.

At a much more mundane level, there is ample evidence today in many companies that financial reporting is less than transparent and that shareholders and the public at large are misled. A good reputation has become an important ingredient in the pursuit of business success. This is no guarantee that companies that pursue ethically acceptable policies will not suffer adversity, and the converse is certainly true. However, companies that pursue a policy of good corporate citizenship will certainly rank highly in the opinion of society.

The identification of ethical issues may present difficulty. Sometimes ethics tends to overlap with personal morality. Sometimes public policy or commercial practice may intrude as well. However, today strong outside interests may intrude as stakeholders, who may well have ulterior objectives, impose challenges and constraints, on many enterprises.

For example, some investment funds purport not to invest in companies that trade in countries where there is civil strife. Their rationale is that the profits generated in such countries are at the expense of the unfortunate citizens or the taxes imposed by the country fuel the conflict. Or consider actions taken by companies that attempt to circumvent economic sanctions or the prohibition on the transfer of highly sensitive intellectual property. These are all ethical issues.

At the corporate level, the list of ethical issues is extensive, including:

- Fraud
- Bribery and corruption
- Misleading advertising
- Unfair competition

Within the companies themselves there are many opportunities for improper behavior which is much less tolerated today than it was a few years ago.

The most devout advocates of appropriate ethical behavior believe that practically every business decision and its implementation has ethical considerations and that no business decision should be taken without considering such implications. Obviously this belief, if extended unrealistically, could seriously hinder the conduct of any business.

Special interest groups often advocate on behalf of their causes. Such groups attempt to couple ethical considerations with the concept of social engineering. These groups include ones that rail against world poverty by attempting to disrupt meetings of the World Trade Organization, for example.

Directors must consider precisely what constitutes acceptable ethical behavior for the company and how it should be applied. They must attempt to achieve a balance between operating in a permissible, but nevertheless profitable, mode and, at the same time, fulfilling the company's social responsibilities to the community and society as a whole.

GOOD CORPORATE CITIZENSHIP

According to Peter Morgan, then director general of the UK Institute of Directors:

> Ethics can be defined as applied morality, concentrating on what to do and how to do it rather than the whys and whethers. Tackled from this standpoint, the close convergence between the behaviour required to run an ethical business and a profitable business—a "good" business in both senses—becomes very clear. Three aspects are especially important:
>
> - No business can be good by accident; objectives must be defined, policies and strategies devised, responsibilities assigned and performance monitored.
> - No business can be good unless it pays the most scrupulous attention to the needs and aspirations of all the people associated with it or affected by it.
> - No business can be good unless it is properly led by its board.[1]

The major conflict most companies seem to wrestle with is reconciling ethical behavior with conducting a business efficiently and profitably. Many people seem to feel that these objectives are at odds with each other. When operating in a competitive environment, directors often are tempted to go one better than the competition; this may lead to cutting corners to the extent that recognized standards of behavior may be compromised.

To reach a better understanding of good corporate citizenship, directors have to understand something about the competing constituencies challenging the free enterprise business. Few would dispute the need to behave honorably in developing markets and competing for business. In fact, most jurisdictions have introduced laws that clearly lay down the standards to which companies must comply. For example, Canada now has a federal law that prohibits Canadian companies offering bribes or being involved in any form of corrupt practice, wherever in the world they operate. In most parts of Europe, there have been major clampdowns on financial practices to avoid under-the-table payments or money laundering. Even traditional barriers of secrecy in such havens as Switzerland and various offshore islands have been found susceptible to official inquiry, although some overzealous bureaucracies have reportedly abused this facility.

Companies also have obligations to ensure that their products are safe and do not either offer or contribute to health or safety hazards. The recent Bridgestone/Firestone tire recalls and the Union Carbide leak in India are two instances of major misfortune.

Major pharmaceutical and chemical companies involved in mining or producing pollution are only too aware of the need to protect the environment. However, not every country that was a signatory to the Kyoto Accord on reducing greenhouse gases appears to be following the timetable for realistic implementation.

Clearly sound business ethics are not bad for business. Indeed, ethical behavior should be the cornerstone for sensible corporate governance and sound business management. It is also a pragmatic basis for operating the enterprise.

Who are the relevant stakeholders with an interest in good corporate citizenship? First and foremost must come the companies' shareholders and employees, followed closely by customers, suppliers, the community in which they operate, and society at large.

What does good corporate citizenship involve? This is sometimes less evident, but prominent among the needs are:

- Truthfulness
- A compassionate business philosophy (which should be publicized)
- Honesty and candor in dealings with customers, suppliers, the community in which the company operates
- Communicating readily and with a prudent degree of openness
- Approachability and not being unnecessarily secretive
- Full compliance with the spirit and application of all appropriate legislation, regulations, and business practices

There is little doubt that ethical issues do affect decision making. However, the need to make a profit must be balanced with ethical actions, and policies that take account of all stakeholders must be developed. Above all, the board should provide leadership and not avoid making decisions regarding ethical matters. There does seem to be a link between those companies that make a formal ethical commitment to their stakeholders and their overall performance. In other words, the best-performing companies also seem to demonstrate the highest levels of good corporate citizenship.

ETHICS AND THE LAW

Recent Canadian legislation that prohibits companies from corrupt practices, such as offering bribes or secret commissions, has been mentioned already. Such corrupt behavior seems endemic in certain parts of the world.

Several other ethical areas much closer to home require particular attention. These include the areas of insider trading, conflicts of interest, undisclosed benefits, breaching the rules of confidentiality, unfair competition, and price fixing.

Directors in particular have various obligations to disclose matters that may produce a conflict of interest. For example, they must disclose financial interests in any holding, subsidiary, or associated company as well as in the company itself. They must also disclose any interest in any contract, transaction, or arrangement with the company. The context of interest includes any related party, such as family or business associate.

As a general guide, conflicts of interest may arise where a director:

- Makes a decision or performs an act motivated by other or additional considerations than that which may be considered in the best interests of the corporation. This is described as acting for collateral purpose. In such circumstances, the exercise of such powers can lead to an accusation of breach of trust, which is considered an offense under the Criminal Code.
- Personally contracts with his corporation, or where he is a director of two corporations that are contracting (or connected in some way) with each other.
- Learns of an opportunity for profit that may be valuable to her personally or to her corporation. These situations are described

as the doctrine of corporate opportunity. Insider trading usually falls into this category.

The definition of undisclosed benefits covers the receipt of all material benefits (including those in kind) from the organization. These should be dealt with in an open manner, disclosed in the annual report if a listed company, and include material contracts and any other arrangement that has a material value. The use of the word "material" is deliberate because it is sometimes a matter of judgment as to when disclosure is necessary. In general, the definition should include benefits or contracts that are large enough in relation to the affairs of the corporation that the company's auditors would want such information to appear in the notes to the financial statements.

Directors also have a responsibility to ensure that they do not take advantage of knowledge that is not in the public domain in relation to share dealings, either by themselves or by parties connected in some manner to them. Taking advantage of such knowledge is defined as both potentially making a profit that is not generally available to others, e.g., the public, and/or divulging information in order that others may potentially make a profit (or avoid a loss). Increasingly stringent obligations are placed on companies to make timely and accurate disclosure of any information that could affect a stock price. The utmost care must be taken not to discriminate between investors. Consider the case of Northern Telecom, whose share price dropped early in 2001 after information regarding likely substantially reduced sales and profitability was leaked to customers of a particular stockbroker prior to the general announcement.

The provision of forward-looking information (i.e., projections and predictions) is an area of confusion. Companies must make such public pronouncements in good faith and on the basis of supportable calculation *at the time the forecast is made*. Companies do not have to adhere to a standard of infallible accuracy, but the prediction must be made in good faith according to the best sources of information available at the time. Furthermore, if the company becomes aware that such predictions are no longer valid, it has an obligation to make public such revised information as soon as it can be validated.

With the explosion in information technology and the warp speed of the Internet, conveying information at the touch of a button has become very easy. An article on cybercrime suggests that more than half of the companies listed on the Financial Times Stock Exchange 1000 index have suffered losses due to Internet abuse.[2] According to one unsubstantiated estimate, up to one-third of the staff at the companies have intentionally, but perhaps unwittingly in some instances, sent confidential files to third parties.

One of the most valuable resources that a company possesses is its intellectual property: its customer lists, its databases, its word processing files, its accounts, plus any trademarks, designs, patents, proprietary formulae, and recipes. The integrity of this information is of paramount importance, and boards must insist that guidelines and procedures are in place to safeguard these assets. One technique to safeguard intellectual property is to have all employees and other people/organizations involved with the company (e.g., suppliers and subcontractors) who may have access to its sensitive information sign comprehensive and legally binding confidentiality agreements. The temptation to engage in any practice that may be classified as corporate espionage, including hiring staff specifically to gain access to highly sensitive competitor information, is actively to be discouraged.

Fairly comprehensive legislation covers the fields of unfair competition and price fixing. Readers are advised to seek qualified legal advice on such matters.

The role of the board, and in particular that of the chairman, is to ensure that management is aware of the risks and the ethical considerations involved in the operation of the business, and have effective procedures in place to monitor the situation and avoid problems arising. Directors in particular must follow written and clearly understood guidelines regarding their own ethical behavior. The chairman must provide the necessary supervision at this level.

Regarding the ethical behavior of chairmen themselves, it is useful for a small committee of senior directors, often the nominating committee or corporate governance committee, to provide the appropriate oversight, counsel and advice where necessary.

ETHICS AND COMPETITION

It has been said that one of the foundations of ethical behavior is trust, and a company's reputation depends on how it deals with its various relationships. A good example is the way in which a company handles its banking and other financial relationships, how it negotiates its borrowings and discharges its debts. One successful businessman in the real estate market dealt simultaneously with several banks, in good times often playing one off another to secure the best terms. He had two mantras in his dealings: Never spring surprises, and always repay when you say you will. Sometimes this meant juggling funds between banks, but he always paid off his debts on time—even if he borrowed the money again immediately afterward. But his reputation remained intact.

But how should the competition be dealt with? The chairman of a major international oil company was convinced that the single most important factor was the level of customer service. Provide this better than anyone else, and price becomes secondary. As he had chaired this successful company for several years, one must assume he knew what he was talking about.

Others suggest that recognizing other stakeholder interests provides a company with an advantage, particularly in international situations. How a company deals with communities, provides ancillary services that benefit employees' families, recognizes the rights of minorities and the disadvantaged, is sometimes disproportionately important both to the company and to the stakeholders involved.

However, boards must decide whether such courses of action are practicable in bringing overall benefit, or whether they will affect the level of potential profitability. Will one group benefit to the disadvantage of another, say shareholders? Such situations sometimes involve a company, its management, and its board in the political arena. The excessive award of share options, for example, and the subsequent dilution of the stock of other shareholders may fall into this category.

Then there is the whole question of influencing government. Legislation regarding lobbying is now such that this parlaying of influence has become a lot more open. Lobbyists, or those who promote positions on behalf of a company, are publicly disclosed today. Information on how successful they are is less likely to be made accessible. In the case of a potential major aircraft sale to another country, export guarantees made a substantial difference in the value of the purchaser's bid. The federal government agreed to the guarantee, and widespread negative publicity arose regarding the potential expense that taxpayers could incur. A more recent example is the dispute regarding the import of softwood lumber from Canada into the United States. One trade lobby alleges unfair subsidies, while the other suggests inefficient production methods. The lobbies are reported to have spent tens of millions of dollars in advancing their respective causes with governments.

Those who choose to be involved in influencing government—not only within their country but overseas as well—must walk the fine line between corporate and community benefit and potentially unfair trade practice. The boundary is sometimes extremely difficult to define. The judgment to be exercised in deciding whether a company is pursuing a trade practice unfairly has to relate to the corporation's place in society and the long-term interests of the organization as a whole. It is impossible to be all things to all people, but a corporation can attempt to be fair, reliable, and a good corporate citizen.

SPONSORSHIPS AND CHARITIES

The doctrine of modern corporate responsibility now dictates that a company cannot ignore being a good neighbor, a good corporate constituent, a participant in the overall social fabric of society. Charitable giving has been around a long time, almost as long as the word "philanthropy." Many world-famous companies, particularly those connected with the Quaker families in England, have contributed enormous sums to the community. In some instances, whole villages or townships grew up around a particular family enterprise, such as Cadbury Chocolate, Coleman's Mustard, Clark's Shoes, Lever Brothers, and the Bata Shoe Company.

Originally, such generosity was described as paternalism, because it tended to relate to the provision of services for the workforce connected with the company. These provisions evolved into sickness benefits and rudimentary health care long before state-run schemes appeared. Today most reputable companies are involved in some form of community sponsorship or provision of social benefits to employees and their families.

In 1997 it was estimated that corporate giving in the United States was in the range of $7 to $9 billion. Commentators have remarked that all this money is given away without shareholder approval, and usually without any disclosure either. Current accounting rules do not mandate disclosure of charitable donations, although the fact of sponsorship often is in the public domain even though the amount may not be. If the money is donated without any significant form of quid pro quo, such as major publicity or advertising in some form, the donor corporation receives little in return that will benefit either it or the shareholders. Where is accountability? The board of directors must consider such questions carefully. A balance must be found between protecting company assets and giving back to the community.

The Canada Customs and Revenue Agency estimates that today around 70,000 organizations have been granted charitable status in Canada. Quite a few of these are endowments or foundations set up specifically to assist in a wide variety of philanthropic causes. However, corporations receive major benefits from sponsoring charitable and community projects. Indeed, creating visibility and influencing potential customers can be quite cost-effective in terms of marketing dollars. The establishment of charitable foundations can provide certain tax advantages to the corporation, but specialist advice before doing so is mandatory, particularly in the United States, where the situation is even more complex.

Companies must be both transparent and professional in handling sponsorships or charitable activities. Not only must board policies be established and rigorously enforced, but these policies must relate directly to the likely benefit to the corporation. With the cutbacks in government spending, private sector involvement in funding anything, from building hospitals to promoting sporting and cultural events, is increasing dramatically. The demands on the corporate sector are many times what the corporate sector can likely afford.

The only criterion for participating in community affairs by means of sponsorships and charitable contributions is for such participation to be part of running a sound and sensible business operation. If helping the community is good for business, it follows that incorporating a reasonable and affordable policy of philanthropic generosity can make sound business sense as well.

A final way of contributing to the public good can involve the physical resources of the company, including that of its staff. Many companies now involve their personnel in charitable giving; United Way in North America is a prime example. Other enterprises encourage employees to volunteer their time, and some even allocate people temporarily to help organize the implementation of specific charitable events. Donating in kind should not be overlooked as a practicable alternative to financial contributions.

CODE OF CONDUCT

It is highly recommended that companies consider instituting a written code of conduct for the conduct of its business and the behavior of its employees. The code should instill a commitment to act with integrity and promote the fact that good corporate citizenship is beneficial to company financial performance.

Social, ethical, and environmental issues are an important part of the board's agenda and will become more so. The board, specifically independent directors, plays a significant role in addressing ethical issues. Ethical issues should not cause argument or disagreement at board meetings as they should be considered as a fundamental principle in the conduct of business.

Many codes of ethical practice have been published. In devising a code appropriate to the corporation, the following important areas should be considered:

- Policies regarding the organization, including risk management and financial reporting
- Relations with customers, suppliers, and consumers
- Community relations
- Employee practices and standards of behavior
- Personal behavior and conduct
- Relations with shareholders and policies regarding disclosure
- Relations with stakeholders and fair dealing
- Policies regarding health and safety, the environment, natural resources, and society

International mining and natural resource company Rio Tinto has declared in its "Statement of Business Practice" dated 1998 that:

Wherever we operate, we work as closely as possible with our hosts, respecting laws and customs, minimising adverse impacts and ensuring a transfer of benefits and enhancement of opportunities. We believe our competitiveness and future success depend not only on our employees and the quality and diversity of our assets but also on our record as good neighbours and partners around the world.[3]

Lord Holme of Cheltenham, at the time director of External Affairs and Human Resources for Rio Tinto, maintained that larger companies have the responsibility to improve standards as they have the strength to resist bribery and corruption.

They also have the resources to improve performance and can sustain a longer time scale beyond just this year's financial results. . . . Larger companies must be more accountable when demonstrating that they adhere to these higher standards. There is a significant difference in my mind between responsibility and accountability. Rio's standards are not imposed by the board. They are a summation of actual practices and policies that have become "owned" by management. Accountability, on the one hand, means transparency within the sensible confines of competition—one cannot reveal absolutely everything. I do not believe it would be practicable to have one international code of practice for social responsibility, otherwise that would tend to relate to the lowest common denominator. On the other hand, companies (and governments) must eventually come to terms with external verification. The key question is: how does a company make itself a good corporate citizen? The best codes of practice come from values of employees who work for good companies.[4]

Rio Tinto states that its annual and half-yearly reports and financial statements are prepared for shareholders on all aspects of business performance, in compliance with the appropriate regulations and undertakings in the various jurisdictions where company shares are listed. Rio Tinto claims to go further than mere statutory compliance in several areas:

> On health and safety and the environment, for example, we not only review in our annual report to shareholders major aspects of policy and practice, but we also publish a separate health, safety and environment report, extending the quality and quantity of the information we provide. . . . Rio Tinto recognizes that excellence in managing health, safety and environmental responsibilities is essential for long-term success. Through effective management practices the Group aims to ensure the health and safety of it employees, to minimise any adverse impacts its activities may have on the environment, and to make a positive contribution to local community life. . . . We mandate that operations should ensure efficient use of energy, water and other materials and pursue implementation of pollution prevention programs, conduct regular audits . . . and evaluate risks associated with activities and products and take appropriate action to minimise appropriate risks.

Finally, under the heading of accounting standards and internal financial control, Rio Tinto indicates that financial statements are prepared for each financial period:

> [W]hich give a true and fair view of our affairs at the end of the financial period and of the profit and loss for that period. For this purpose, accounting policies are used and applied consistently, rea-

sonable and prudent judgments are made and applicable accounting standards are followed. Systems of internal financial control are in operation which are designed to provide reasonable but not absolute, assurance regarding first, the safeguard of assets against unauthorized use or disposition; and secondly, the maintenance of proper accounting records and the reliability of financial information used within the business or for publication.[5]

Many readers will concur that these statements reflect good ethical practice. What made Rio Tinto stand out in 1998 was that it went public decisively with its statements of intention and practice. It is prepared to stand up and be counted and, in so doing, allows itself precious little leeway to diverge from the high standards it has set.

The Australian Institute of Company Directors took a major step forward in its Vision 2000 mission by publishing a Code of Conduct for Directors. Intended to promote the highest ethical and professional standards in directorship of Australian companies, the code provides guidance to assist directors in carrying out their duties and responsibilities. Perhaps more important, the code defines standards of professional conduct that the institute expects of its members.

The code is phrased in such a way that it is equally relevant to directors of listed companies, small proprietary companies, crown corporations, and not-for-profit organizations. Interestingly, the institute even managed to put some teeth into the code: "From January, 1997 Fellows of the Institute [the highest grade] will be subject to disciplinary action for failure to comply with the principals contained in the code." For a powerful organization with a current membership in excess of 16,500 business leaders in a country with 20 million population [all 2002 figures], this promises to be quite a sanction on unacceptable corporate behavior.

The code emphasizes the self-regulatory approach to the conduct of business. It accepts that there will always be a requirement for regulation to establish a control framework to meet society's business expectations. It also expects the level of regulatory control over business to be proportionate to the trust shown by society in the willingness of business to meet these expectations. In other words, if companies want less government oversight, they must demonstrate that they can keep their own house in order.

The full code is shown in Exhibit 10.1.

Exhibit 10.1   Code of Conduct for Corporate Directors.

1. A director must act honestly, in good faith and in the best interests of the company as a whole.

2. A director has a duty to use care and diligence in fulfilling the functions of office and exercising the powers attached to that office.

3. A director must use the powers of office for a proper purpose, in the best interests of the company as a whole.

4. A director must recognize that the primary responsibility is to the company's shareholders as a whole but should, where appropriate, have regards for the interests of all stakeholders of the company.

5. A director must not make improper use of information acquired as a director.

6. A director must not take improper advantage of the position of director.

7. A director must not allow personal interests, or the interests of an associated person, to conflict with the interests of the company.

8. A director has an obligation to be independent in judgment and actions and to take all reasonable steps to be satisfied as to the soundness of decisions taken by the board of directors.

9. Confidential information received by a director in the course of the exercise of directorial duties remains the property of the company from which it was obtained and it is improper to disclose it, or allow it to be disclosed, unless the disclosure has been authorized by that company, or the person from whom the information is provided, or is required by law.

10. A director should not engage in conduct likely to bring discredit upon the company.

11. A director has an obligation, at all times, to comply with the spirit, as well as the letter, of the law and the principles of this Code.

Source: Abstracted from *Code of Conduct* (Australian Institute of Company Directors, 1996), p. 7. Used with permission.

CHAPTER 11

Public Affairs

Efficiency is doing things right.
Effectiveness is doing the right thing.

—Zig Ziglar, *Quotes for Everyday Inspiration,*
CCH Canadian

ESTABLISHING A POLICY

It is said that those who control the propaganda machine control the country. The first targets of those planning coups are the radio and TV stations. The ability to manipulate information is disproportionately powerful and effective.

Translate this into the business context and at one end of the spectrum we have the relatively respectable fields of promotion, public relations, and advertising. At the other end are some of the more vicious negative publicity campaigns evident in some U.S. elections. Just a few short years ago, overt comparisons with competitive products or services were considered ungentlemanly, perhaps even unethical. No longer.

The heading "public affairs" encompasses public policy, public relations, lobbying, crisis management, community relations, social advocacy, stockholder communications, advertising, and many other activities that derive from, or influence, the public persona of the corporation. Public affairs embraces the entire concepts of image, reputation, and influence—and through them, of course, the bottom line.

Although cloaked in modern terminology, these activities are directed toward the company surviving, succeeding, and prospering just as much a good corporate citizenship and altruism. What has to be achieved is an appropriate and prudent balance between the two.

What are the benefits from promoting a positive image—satisfied customers, loyal employees, industry status, and maybe even friendly attention from the media? Public relations practitioners will argue, with some justification, that a company needs constantly to work on its public image, promoting the positive and maintaining its market niche.

What of the downside? What about the damage that can be caused by disgruntled employees, dissatisfied customers, special interest groups, and desperate competitors? Even worse, what about the disaster scenario that the makers of Tylenol faced down a number of years ago?

How does this challenge affect today's board of directors? Most boards are aware of the need for product marketing, company image, employee morale, and so on. How many boards are prepared to deal with negative situations, some of which may occur without warning? The first essential is to have certain specific directors or senior employees designated as company spokesmen in defined situations. The chairman often must represent the company in the most important situations that arise. It is therefore an essential part of their job specifications that chairmen learn how to perform this role of spokesperson effectively in a crisis. Some of the more sophisticated larger companies have a designated "war room" where key players assemble immediately after crisis strikes.

Scripts can be prepared for some of the more predictable scenarios and, at least yearly, a day or more should be spent in rehearsing action plans. What kind of problems can a board anticipate? These can range widely from a product liability situation, such as the Tylenol tampering scare; through fire, explosion, or other major accident; to an unwelcome takeover bid; to employee discontent or even misleading advertising by a competitor. It is vital to preselect any additional resources—such as outside legal support, public relations practitioners, and so on—whose services may be required in a hurry.

The New Zealand Institute of Directors listed some of the more common situations that can be planned for and rehearsed ahead of time in an October 1994 article. These situations include, among others:

- Would you know what to do if, rightly or wrongly, your product was found to be faulty or dangerous?

- Do you have a plan of action if some kind of campaign is launched against you or your industry?
- If you are, or can become, vulnerable to takeover, are you geared quickly to mobilise resources to gain maximum benefit from media coverage, shareholder loyalty, goodwill, etc?
- Are you set up to hear about a potentially damaging article or story before it is published or broadcast?
- Do employees have to rely on an informal unreliable "grapevine" for information on what is happening in the organization and, conversely, do you have a way of finding out what employees think of the organization's management, and of their immediate superiors?
- How much damage can be done to your organization by an ill-informed attack by a politician, public figure (or a journalist)?[1]

Crisis situations are discussed in more detail later in this chapter. How many directors realize the devastating effect of something going wrong, often something that is outside the company's control? Some of the more obvious crises, such as product tampering or failure, can be predicted more precisely as a potential disaster scenario and contingency action can be planned. However, it has been estimated that should a company's computer system be destroyed, by fire for example, and a sound and comprehensive backup system is not available almost immediately, an average company has little more than two and a half to three days to resume satisfactory operations before it experiences some permanent damage.

To quote the Boy Scout motto: "Be prepared!" Many companies tend to deal with communications reactively. Unless a company is set up to handle adverse situations, by the time it learns how to do so, it may almost be too late.

BUSINESS AND GOVERNMENT

In the business environment of the twenty-first century, where globalization and international competition prevails, companies must ensure that they conduct their affairs in a way that provides the greatest opportunities for success. Today many governments offer a variety of incentives, ranging from export guarantees to subsidies and financial support, to create employment in various locales. In such cases, it is not unprincipled to take advantage of such opportunities where they can provide a competitive edge, providing the firm still behaves responsibly. (But see also Chapter 10.)

Companies must attempt to be informed of existing and likely developments that can be of benefit to them. There are many ways companies can do this, not the least of which is maintaining regular contact with government agencies that may be of assistance. A company that is not aware cannot gain an advantage.

Although lobbying is regulated today to the extent that lobbyists must register both federally and in other jurisdictions, and, if acting in a consultancy capacity, they must identify their clients, many organizations still consider the use of lobbyists very worthwhile. The power of the National Rifle Association, or gun lobby, in the United States, or of the tobacco manufacturers indicates the influence that can be exerted on legislators. Ethical pharmaceutical manufacturers in Canada have been successful in their threats to reduce funding for Canadian-based research and development as a means of obtaining extended patent protection for their drugs.

Even at the local level, a company that wishes, say, to construct a new plant and requires local municipal support to provide infrastructure services has to go through a whole series of public inquiries and appeals before it receives final consent.

In another context, both state/provincial and federal levels of government strongly support trade missions to various countries and provide strong local support to obtain business or generate joint venture agreements.

Many programs are available to assist smaller and medium-size businesses with initial research and development, marketing and promotion, even job creation. Broadly speaking, there is something likely to be of benefit to almost every type of entrepreneurial enterprise. The problem is to make sure that the company has all the currently available information and is not afraid to take advantage of the opportunities obtainable. Governments have money to spend. The secret is enabling the company to benefit from it.

Larger companies tend to appoint vice presidents to assume responsibility for government and public affairs; smaller companies must rely more on their CEOs and board members. The chairman in particular often has a key role to play. Larger companies can afford to invite well-connected ex-politicians and retired bureaucrats with the necessary contacts to join their boards. Smaller enterprises must be resourceful and use their ingenuity to compensate for their inability to do so.

With global competition and the reduction in trade barriers, companies must be aware of the threat that offshore producers can gain access to the domestic market. Companies must ensure that policies are in place to assist them ethically to remain competitive in such situations. While blatant subsidies or other unilateral financial incentives are contrary to various international agreements, providing education, developing new technologies, and using beneficial taxation opportunities to increase, for example, productivity, and to remove any internal trade constraints are all accepted methods to ensure a firm's prosperity.

The key is not so much access to the marketplace but competitiveness. Competitiveness is not confined simply to price; it refers equally, if not more importantly, to services such as quality, delivery, and customer relationships. Directors must be strongly proactive in supporting the need to remain competitive and, if necessary, in convincing policymakers of the need for their support. In some instances, costs created by government are included in the cost of doing business. However, government often has more than one choice as to how to raise taxation revenue, and directors must be outspoken in their attempts to convince legislators of the need to survive in a competitive environment. As James Gillies puts it succinctly in *Boardroom Renaissance*:

> The change in the international marketplace means that . . . two of the most obvious and important priorities for directors must be:
>
> 1. To adopt pro-active strategies to work with all levels of government to put in place policies that ensure that Canadian firms are not at a competitive disadvantage because of domestic economic policies with firms domiciled in other jurisdictions; and,
> 2. To ensure that the enterprises for which they are responsible are managed strategically within the context of the global marketplace.[2]

SHAREHOLDERS, STAKEHOLDERS, AND SOCIAL RESPONSIBILITY

Articles have appeared in the media from time to time expressing as "indecent" or "immoral" the level of executive pay. In fact, shareholder activists have attempted, and sometimes succeeded, in placing on the agenda for the annual meeting of some Canadian chartered banks resolutions limiting the pay for top executives to a much more modest multiple of the average employee's remuneration.

While there may be explanations why relatively few but publicly prominent executives do receive pay packets in the multimillion-dollar range, the fact is that public perception regarding this level of remuneration plays an important role. This has been one of the reasons for increased shareholder activism in recent years.

Yves Michaud, journalist, politician, Quebec sovereigntist, and shareholder activist has stated:

> [In reality,] a very large publicly held company (that is, one with shares widely held and with no one controlling shareholder) is run by its officers. A board of directors frequently serves as little more than a "rubber stamp" to approve decisions made by the officers. . . . From this point onwards, corporate governance has gone mainstream. Shareholders, boards and managers must recognize that it is not simply a distraction or an irrelevant detail, but rather an essential part of asset management for managers and directors. At the same time, [it is also] a highly competitive investment strategy for shareholders. No longer [is it] an add-on to public pension alternatives, if any. Nor is it about social policy. Corporate governance is an essential part of the agenda for the broadest range of investors, directors and managers.
>
> Time and experience will demonstrate that investors, whether large institutions or individual shareholders, can protect and enhance the value of their investments through shareholder activism, at least as cost-effectively as through trading, and often more so.[3]

A year later, Terence Corcoran, then recently appointed as editor of the *Financial Post*, took an opposing view, saying:

> I think that it is important to put this debate into a much broader and general context. What Mr. Michaud represents is one of the two separate streams of corporate activism in Canada. Their objective is to destroy the corporation as we know it. Their objective is to subvert the concept of the corporation and abolish the basic foundations of law and tradition of big corporations which have created the greatest economic growth and prosperity the world has ever seen.
>
> A corporation is a free, volunteer association of shareholders. Directly or indirectly, these shareholders are ultimately individuals. The right to organize a corporation is an extension of the rights of individuals to associate and to agree among themselves to invest their

money and to act as a group under conditions that they devise and accept. . . .

There are two main subversive theories that Mr. Michaud and others are trying to import and impose upon our corporations. One is the corporate democracy theory that Mr. Michaud specifically represents. In this line of argument, the corporation is the equivalent of a democratic government and shareholders, unlike voters and citizens in a democracy, are rulers of these kingdoms. Power is supposed to be exercised by democratic vote at annual meetings or even more frequently. As we have seen by Mr. Michaud's activities with the banks, just about anything could be put to shareholder referendum: executive salaries, the sex of board members, social policies, business plans, lending policies, [all] could be determined by shareholder vote. Mr. Michaud has proposed board appointment techniques which allow small groups of shareholders to elect board members. The effect would be to turn boards into faction-driven miniature parliaments. . . .

At the other end of the spectrum, also chewing away at the heart of our corporate structure is the stakeholder movement. The stakeholder movement holds that corporations should be run for all stakeholders, not just shareholders. The objective of the stakeholder movement is to force companies by law and regulation to broaden their focus to include any other group than shareholders. Stakeholderism or the corporate ethics movement would make managers legally accountable to a broader range of people. Profits would become secondary. Nobody really knows what a stakeholder really is. It is an ambiguous or holistic concept that has no real meaning. . . . [4]

These two presentations demonstrate rather well the sense of extremism that has come to pass in recent years. Readers may have some sympathy or distaste for the views expressed. But the views do indicate the polarization that exists and how essential it is for companies to set in place public policies that both react to and, where necessary, accommodate these extremes.

Michaud has been unbelievably successful in a few of his proposals. Major Canadian banks have placed certain of his proposals on their annual meeting agenda of their own accord and in a few instances even have implemented them. So it can be argued that some good comes out of radical views. But it is hoped that there could be a better way.

Corcoran, on the other hand, sounds a warning that we would do well to heed. Again, while readers may not agree with all of his remarks, his statement does emphasize the need to balance corporate policy, as it pertains to stakeholders and others, rather carefully. Many boards may feel that they are not large enough to merit attention from outsiders, but labor unrest or environmental concerns can affect companies of virtually any size.

DEALING WITH THE MEDIA

It may be hard to believe that a newspaper editor states stories about sex, scandal, or illegalities often take precedence over hard news, but one said precisely that a few years ago. We suppose it sells more newspapers. Another reporter interviewing a director for a TV program on governance quickly departed from the prepared script when she got a whiff of something that may have the potential to titillate viewers. Another editor chose to print only a partial response to a reporter's questions, with the result that the context was changed completely.

These real-life instances may seem to be an indictment of the media, but they are facts of life. For example, despite assurances to the contrary, there is no such thing as "off the record" or "in confidence." The only thing a person can expect in such circumstances is for the ensuing article to refer to an "undisclosed source." And reporters tend to grant this privilege to retain access to a future potential source of information rather than to protect the innocent.

Today's media sometimes seems irresponsible, manipulating news for the benefit of readers/viewers rather than presenting unvarnished facts. But this is what journalism today seems to be all about. And to be fair, without such an approach, a lot of material would be rather dry, even though the provider of such news may feel it of paramount importance.

Journalism today is all about numbers: of readers, of viewers. From this evolves potential advertising revenue and a disproportionate effect on the bottom line. Always be aware of what influences the media. At the same time, always realize that there is constant, and often intense, competition for the available space, either in the publication or on the air waves and on the Internet.

What policies should companies establish for dealing with the media?

- A successful businessman once stated that if you want to exhibit your washing on the line, make sure it's all clean. Information cannot be provided selectively. If a company opens the door to the media, it had better be sure that it will be comfortable with

161

everything that is revealed. That means everything relating to the item of news in question, not necessarily something completely unrelated.

- If the news is not good—for example, poor operating results, a labor dispute, even financial difficulties—consult an expert before saying anything. Many professional advisors have a gift for presenting information in such a way that the media tend (only tend—it's not absolute) to take it at face value without going around or beneath the news for some ulterior motive.
- If it is good news, make sure that it is presented with sufficient humility so that the media do not think that the company is attempting to obtain free publicity—even though that may be the result. In other words, the criterion of newsworthiness must be paramount.
- If the event involves a crisis—potential, real, unexpected, or whatever—again seek immediate expert advice. Do not attempt to meet the media unless fully prepared with a frank and forthright explanation that has a positive, rather than negative, spin attached.
- Credible access to the media is limited. Do not waste time in calling press conferences for anything other than hard, and interesting, news. Even though members of the media may have expressed the intention of attending yesterday, today's hot potatoes may change their good intentions.
- Select those members of the media to inform carefully. Relationships are everything. They make take ages to build and minutes to destroy. Be selective and be consistent. Do not attempt to play favorites, because the media rarely gives out favors in return; reporters have to be hard-nosed in obtaining news or their job may be on the line.
- Perhaps most important, make sure that whoever is chosen to represent the company to the media is skilled in presentation, chooses her words very carefully so as to avoid misrepresentation and being taken out of context, and comes across as being frank and honest. Excellent trainers can school senior executives in presentation skills and in avoiding interviewers' traps. Follow their advice.

Items that are likely to attract media attention vary dramatically according to the enterprise. The focus here is on preparedness. There are some items the board should consider key for their agenda.

Some time ago, a company bought another in an allied industry. There was a significant element of goodwill in the purchase because the purchased company's product line complemented the acquirer's. After the formalities were completed, the president of the acquiring company visited the purchased company's offices and plant and addressed the assembled employees. He greeted them and welcomed them to the combined organization. Hoping to reassure any concerns that they may have had, he announced that everyone's job was secure "for at least three months." He did not seem to understand why most of the best workers and key employees found alternative work before the three months was up.

Should the president have said anything? He presumed, probably accurately, that job security would be one of the key questions on everyone's mind. Where he went wrong was not in raising the matter, but in expressing himself in a way that led people to assume the worst. A lot of the expensive goodwill went out of the window. The lesson here is that what one says and how one says it is of vital importance.

The board should consider, as a regular part of its agenda, the many areas that could affect the company and potentially attract the attention of the media. Obviously, it is preferable to be proactive where appropriate rather than to be reactive, which could place one at a disadvantage. Sometimes there may be little choice. Some items to address may include:

- Those items that must be disclosed by regulation which may attract media attention
- The company's social performance and responsibilities, including labor relations
- The company's ethical performance as set out in Chapter 10
- Any developments in the company's policies and practices relating to environmental considerations, community involvement, health and safety, customer service, product safety, and the like that may influence the company's image or status
- Management's diligence in identifying situations that may place the company at risk in any of the foregoing situations
- How communications—those mandated by law, such as annual reports, as well as non-mandated ones—are made and monitored; how the company uses expert advice
- The company's consideration, preparation for, and rehearsal of any potential crisis situations, particularly how it should handle these events and who presents information to the media

HANDLING A CRISIS

Perhaps the most common crisis a board encounters is one involving management. One company that relied greatly on its president was almost unable to cope when he died in a plane crash. There was no planned backup; no designated succession; not even a deputy who could step into the breach on a temporary basis other than the chairman who, unfortunately, was out of touch with current activities.

Much less dramatic personnel events, ranging from sudden illness or death of a pivotal individual to a competitor attracting a key employee away from the company, can cause management crises. Not only is the person lost; his or her knowledge base is also gone, and that knowledge base may be hard to replace in the short term. A company's knowledge base, particularly in a service-oriented industry, is disproportionately valuable.

Companies must recognize that no one is indispensable, and that there should always exist contingency plans covering various eventualities. However, it is important to recognize that sometimes unexpected situations do occur that the media learn about. Before anyone realizes it, everyone from the banks, the stock exchange, and customers and suppliers become concerned. The company's credit rating may be affected, as may be its share price, and business could be anything from minimally to severely affected.

Such situations can arise if an unexpected takeover bid occurs, particularly if it is considered hostile. The takeover bid by Trilogy (a front for the Indigo chain of bookstores) for Chapters Books forced Chapters to take a variety of precipitous actions, with varying degrees of success, that emphasized the company's almost total unpreparedness for such a situation. The experience was, for Chapters, also a public relations failure.

The TransUnion case in 1985 in Delaware, which basically gave rise to the directors' and officers' legal liability crisis of the mid-1980s, was an instance of another public relations disaster.

Patrick Caragata's excellent book, *Business Early Warning Systems,*[5] covers a wide spectrum of crisis situations and how they should be dealt with. The last word in this chapter is reserved for Sir Adrian Cadbury, who writes:

> Boards should be doing more to explain the complexities which lie behind major business decisions. Interest groups aim to simplify all the arguments down to an issue of right or wrong. If decisions were

as straightforward as that, boards would not need to spend much time on them. The problem for an interest group is that once the wider implications of business decisions are brought into the discussion, the narrow pre-occupation which gives the group its cohesion is weakened. . . .

Not all the interests involved will have organized groups to represent them. For a company to go along with the demands of the most vocal or best organized pressure group could be an easy way out of resolving a difficult conflict of interest, rather than an expression of social responsibility.[6]

CHAPTER 12

The Volunteer Board

The nature of men is always the same;
It is their habits that separate them.

—Confucius, *Analects,* ca. 500 B.C.

WHAT DOES "VOLUNTEER" MEAN?

One of the most definitive documents released in recent years in Canada concerning the voluntary sector was *Building on Strength: Improving Governance and Accountability in Canada's Voluntary Sector,* known as the Broadbent Report after its chairman, former federal politician Ed Broadbent. The report was far-reaching in its conclusions and recommendations.

According to the report, the nonprofit sector in Canada consists of approximately 175,000 organizations, slightly over 78,000 of which are registered charities. In total, they have some $90 billion in annual revenues, $109 billion in assets, and employ roughly 9 percent of the country's labor force: 1.3 million people. Taken as a whole, the sector accounts for one-eighth of Canada's gross domestic product. Almost one-third of the working population, some 7.5 million people, did some kind of volunteer work through an organization in 1997, a constantly increasing figure.[1]

Volunteer or not-for-profit activities range from the large charitable sector, through professional, advocacy, trade, secular, religious, sports organizations, and many others to teaching institutions and hospitals. (Note that "not-for-profit" is considered a more accurate term than "nonprofit," which can be taken to imply that activities are not intended to generate a surplus.) In fact, it is estimated that teaching institutions and hospitals represent some 60 percent of the annual revenues of $90 billion mentioned above. The defining element is the fact that not-for-profit organizations enjoy special tax exemptions. Although they do not pay Canadian income tax (except on investment income), not-for-profit organizations are not entitled to offer tax incentives to those who contribute to their work except for registered charitable receipts and work- (or profession-) related membership fees, which are allowed in specific and limited circumstances.

While for-profit activities have been the kernel of this book thus far, the not-for-profit sector is massive. Although many not-for-profits have a small paid staff, some organizations, in particular hospitals and teaching institutions, have huge budgets and employ thousands of people. This fact alone dictates that they, like most volunteer organizations, should be run on sound business principles.

The sad fact is that many of them are not. One commentator is reported to have said that many volunteer boards consist of eclectic individuals with indisputable business acumen, "the majority of whom tend to leave their brains at the door!" If experience is anything to go by, this statement does embrace an element of truth.

There are many reasons for this, the most significant being that volunteer boards tend to rotate frequently and rely on recruitment of talent from a variety of sources, some of which do not necessarily produce the best resources to govern the organization concerned. Another important reason why volunteer boards often do not demonstrate the highest standards of board governance is that the position of chairman (or chief elected officer) is often regarded by the holder by its status rather than by the qualities of leadership demanded of it.

This book cannot provide complete coverage of the volunteer sector. However, there are many organizations that have revenues and budgets equal to or greater than many of those that operate in the for-profit environment as publicly listed companies. Teaching institutions and hospitals are an obvious category. Some charities also operate with annual budgets well in excess of Can$100 million. The Canadian credit union industry (the largest individual organization with assets of well over Can$4 billion) and cooperatives are other major organizations that operate with volunteer boards. Therefore, this chapter focuses on the larger not-for-profit enterprises and relates the duties of the board of directors and its chairman, and on a number of the principles of sound governance that should apply to them.

WHY VOLUNTEER BOARDS ARE SO DIFFERENT

It is too simplistic to state that while for-profit enterprises and their boards maintain a fiduciary relationship with their shareholders, not-for-profit organizations have a parallel fiduciary relationship with their members. The application of accountability in the volunteer sector places much more emphasis on trust, not only to members where this constituency is well defined, but also to the public at large and society in general. Quoting again from the Broadbent report:

> Accountability in the voluntary sector is multi-layered. It means accountability to different audiences, for a variety of activities and outcomes, through many different means. This multidimensional nature is the principal complexity of accountability in the voluntary sector.
>
> Accountability to whom? Voluntary organizations have accountabilities downward, upward, and outward. They are accountable to their beneficiaries or clients, members, volunteers, staff, partners and affiliates, donors and funders, and governments as well as to the general public. But they are accountable in different ways to these constituencies.[2]

In the larger volunteer organizations—those with the greatest number of paid (as against volunteer) staff—one potential governance problem is the fact that staff are there for the long term. They provide the essential continuity. Staff also deal with the minutiae of the business. They know far better than the volunteer directors all the nuances and peculiarities that make the organization tick.

With many of the members rotating on a regular basis, a voluntary board is hard-pressed to maintain the necessary checks and balances and still remain focused on the mission and purpose of the organization. Volunteer boards face fundamental problems in ensuring that the enterprise is run efficiently, effectively, and in the best interests of its "moral ownership," a phrase John Carver has trademarked and emphasized in his books on policy governance.

Not only do volunteer board memberships tend to rotate frequently, but sometimes people occupy the position of chairman for as little as a year before a successor assumes responsibility. In other words, the most senior elected officer, while appointed to a position of prestige, in some organizations has precious little time to stamp his mark on the enterprise before his term of office expires.

This is not always the case. In fact, at many hospitals and teaching institutions in particular, the chairman's term of office extends over several years. In such cases, the chairmen have much greater guidance and leadership opportunities. Sometimes it is extremely difficult to obtain an appropriate balance between a chairman demonstrating positive leadership characteristics without upsetting the organization's tradition of continuity. On one hand, continuity and time to provide leadership and direction is beneficial. On the other hand, retaining the interest and commitment of other volunteers by allowing them to progress through the various elected officer positions to the top of the organization is considered equally important. As suggested, status and prestige sometimes dictate who becomes chairman rather than underlying capabilities and knowledge of best governance practices.

Some large volunteer boards pursue conventional nominating procedures and invite members to join them. Others boards are elected by constituencies representing principle stakeholders. Yet other members just volunteer their time to the cause in question. Such a selection process may achieve the appropriate levels of talent and expertise, but it may not. However, whatever mix of board capabilities are realized, the perception still exists that not-for-profit organizations have to pursue less demanding governance objectives to those that apply to the for-profit sector. Why is this so?

According to some critics, one reason may be that volunteer directors or trustees do not get paid for their time and devotion. Therefore, there is a different level or degree of commitment. Other critics intimate that provided the cause for which the organization exists is met in a reasonable manner—and "reasonable" is rarely defined—there is little need to maintain the much more rigid approach demanded in the for-profit sector. Undoubtedly there are many other justifications. The fact remains that the Broadbent report's definitions of accountability are disproportionately important, and they influence the manner in which volunteer organizations should be conducted.

However, the chairman or chief elected officer of a volunteer organization *should always* maintain the maximum degree of leadership in helping direct the future of the organization in the most effective manner. In this area there is no difference between for-profit and not-for-profit organizations.

SOME COMMON FAILINGS

The volunteer sector is so diverse that it is often difficult to provide specific advice. Consider the kind of challenges that often face not-for-profit boards:

- Failure to clarify sufficiently the mission, vision, purpose, and objectives of the organization
- Failure to define adequately the roles and responsibilities of the board vis-à-vis staff
- Failure to understand what is required to maintain an effective oversight of a not-for-profit organization
- Failure to address properly the needs of the membership and, where different, the "moral owners"
- Failure to gain the full support of members, volunteers, staff, and other participants, such as government, and the community at large

In an organization with an adequate staff infrastructure, the board must remain focused on the organization itself rather than attempt to become involved in service delivery (or micromanagement). In some instances, board members are tempted to stray from their commitment to the organization's mission the farther removed they are from any direct responsibilities.

Another major failing with not-for-profit organizations is the board's inability to remain focused on its fiduciary responsibilities and the need for sound governance practices. Items of trivial importance tend to get disproportionate attention. The agenda becomes much less structured. Financial items, particularly historical reporting, tend to dominate discussion. The committee structure, where it exists, often operates more independently of the board than is desirable from an accountability perspective. Finally, not-for-profit boards consistently seem to react to staff initiatives rather than to act in a proactive manner. This factor alone is symptomatic of a board relegating its strategic role to a much lower level than it should.

Fundamentally, many boards fail to understand what is required to operate a not-for-profit organization. It is comparatively rare to find a situation where the role of the board has been well defined, particularly in relation to the staff's role. Staff members sometimes find it expedient to take problems to the board, when they should deal with them directly, as the problems usually involve operational matters. It is easier to create a gray area of uncertain governance rather than clarify where the decision appropriately resides.

HOW TO "GOVERN" A VOLUNTEER ORGANIZATION

The Complete Guide to Nonprofit Management, produced by Smith, Bucklin & Associates, a leading U.S. association management company, simplifies the roles and responsibilities of what it describes as a governing board. The board's role is:

- Ensuring the mission is carried out.
- Maintaining fiduciary responsibility.
- Contributing to the organization's bottom line.
- Maintaining ethical standards and board confidentiality while recognizing conflicts of interest.
- Respecting and supporting staff, maintaining appropriate lines of communication, and understanding the maintaining of separate roles.
- Respecting other board members.
- Enhancing the public image of the organization.
- Recruiting other volunteers.[3]

In *Boards That Make a Difference,* John Carver sets out a framework within which to organize the thoughts, activities, structure, and relationship of governing boards. He believes the following points are necessary in not-for-profit governance:

- *"Cradle vision"*: A useful framework for governance must hold and support vision in the primary position. There must be systematic encouragement to think the unthinkable and to dream.
- *Explicitly address fundamental values*: The governing board is a guardian of organizational values. Endless decisions about events cannot substitute for deliberations and explicit pronouncements on values.
- *Force an external focus*: Because [volunteer] organizations tend to focus inward, a governance model must intervene to guarantee a market-like external responsiveness.
- *Enable an outcome-driven organizing system*: All functions and decisions are to be made rigorously against the standard of purpose.
- *Separate large issues from small*: A [governance] model should help to differentiate the size of issues.

- *Force forward thinking*: Strategic leadership demands the long-term viewpoint.
- *Enable pro-activity*: Boards should press towards leading, not towards reacting. Such a model would engage boards more in *creating* than in *approving*.
- *Facilitate diversity and unity*: It is important to optimize the richness of diversity in board composition and opinion, yet still assimilate the variety into one voice.
- *Describe relationships to relevant constituencies*: In either a legal or moral sense, directors are usually trustees; they are also, to some extent, accountable to [other stakeholders—and/or "moral owners"]. A model should define these relationships.
- *Define a common basis for discipline*: Boards have a tough time sticking to a job description, being decisive without being impulsive, and keeping discussion to the point.
- *Determine what information is needed*: A model of governance would introduce more precise distinctions about the nature of information needed to govern, avoiding too much, too little, too late and simply wrong information.
- *Balance over-control and under-control*: A model of governance would clarify those aspects of management that need tight versus loose control.
- *Use board time efficiently*: By sorting out what really needs to be done, a model should enable boards to use the precious gift of time more productively.[4]

Carver packaged some sound but conventional policy governance principles so that volunteers find them relatively easy to comprehend and put into practice. He describes the Policy Governance Model in four broad statements:

> Board Leadership requires, above all, that the board provide vision. To do so, the board must first have an adequate vision of its own job. That role is best conceived neither as volunteer-helper nor watchdog but as trustee-owner. Policy Governance is an approach to the job of governing that emphasizes values, vision, empowerment of both board and staff, and the strategic ability to lead leaders.
>
> Observing the principles of the Policy Governance model, a board of directors crafts its values into [written] policies of the four types below. Policies written this way enable to board to focus its wisdom into one central, brief document:
>
> *Ends*. The board defines which human needs are to be met, for whom and at what cost. Written with a long-term perspective, these

mission-related policies embody most of the board's part of long-range [i.e., strategic] planning.

Executive Limitations. The board establishes the *boundaries* of acceptability within which staff methods and activities can responsibly be left to staff. These limiting policies, therefore, apply to staff means rather than ends. [This defines the terms of reference for the chief staff officer and the terms of reference within which he operates. Provided he performs within the envelope of authority delegated to him, in principle he should be left to direct his resources and get on with the job.]

Board-Executive Linkage. The board clarifies the manner in which it delegates authority to staff as well as how it evaluates staff performance on provisions of the Ends and Executive Limitations policies. [This element embraces the reporting and oversight functions.]

Governance Process. The board determines its philosophy, its accountability and specifics of its own job. [In other words, the board defines how it should function.][5]

Many would argue that these points are common sense and just one approach. That may be true, but relatively few volunteer boards seem to follow the model. Therefore, Carver advocates a more rigid definition of roles and responsibilities; that is one way, sometimes considered quite a successful way, to govern a volunteer organization. One word of caution: Each organization is unique. Too rigid a template or too inflexible an interpretation of the Carver principles could be counterproductive unless the specific needs are detailed in an orderly manner and incorporated into the approach.

The term "chief staff officer" is used to denote the most senior paid employee of the not-for-profit organization. In a hospital such a person may be called chief executive officer, as in the for-profit sector. In a charity, he may be called president or executive director. The term "chief staff officer" can encompass these and many other titles.

The policy governance approach is one of many ways not-for-profit organizations can embrace the majority of the required governance elements needed in the volunteer context.

Other defining characteristics of volunteer boards include the likely involvement of the chairman in presenting the public persona. Sometimes different opinions exist as to who is the most appropriate person to deal with advocacy and public representation. On balance, the chief staff person, if carefully selected, is usually the most appropriate person to present the organization's views in public. This person will have the advantage of continuity and likely a more profound knowledge of the organization and the position it should take on certain issues. More important, as one chief staff officer put it succinctly, "I can place my hand in the fire. If it gets burned, the organization has the ability to repudiate, whereas the chief elected officer, and the organization itself, could suffer much more serious embarrassment."

Besides making official presentations on behalf of the organization, the chief elected officer is usually involved with some public events so as to enhance the visibility and prestige of the organization. Careful briefing is invariably a prudent safeguard. As explained earlier, the media sometimes can be difficult to deal with.

In volunteer organizations, board members frequently are recruited for their contacts and abilities in raising funds. Often volunteering time alone is not enough. Organizations need board members' skill in helping to add to the bottom line. Fund-raising is crucial to many voluntary organizations—not only in the charitable sector, but increasingly in the educational and health sectors, due to government progressively shifting many of its former financial responsibilities toward the private sector. Fund-raising activities are not everyone's forte. Therefore, the selection of board members, particularly the chairman, must take into account the comfort level of being involved in fund-raising. Although the amount of funds raised is important, the principles and actions involved in supporting the mission and objectives of the organization remain equally vital.

Apart from the specific emphasis given in this section, the vast majority of the advice given elsewhere in this book applies equally to the activities of the volunteer not-for-profit sector.

LEADERSHIP IS STILL PARAMOUNT

In a volunteer organization, the chairman is responsible for the integrity of the board process. Only chairmen who are able to handle this challenge should be appointed. Significantly more than in a for-profit situation, the volunteer board chairman must be skilled at handling human dynamics, a people person. If not, it may be difficult to retain the interest and commitment of the other volunteers who make up the governing body.

Autocracy, or heavy-handedness, has little place in the volunteer boardroom. The chairman must be able to draw out the best from what is often a diverse medley of abilities and expertise. More than ever, the principle of a board being consensus-driven applies. At the same time, when board members are elected by specific constituencies, the chairman must tread the fine line in ensuring a balanced perspective that takes all constituencies, plus the needs of the organization as a whole, into account.

Some volunteer organizations, in recognizing the assortment of special interests, try to select a chairman who acts more as a referee than a leader. Such a person shies away from confrontation. Unfortunately, results often are comparable to a lowest common denominator rather than to the highest common factor. This scaling down the quality of decision making is not encouraged. In fact, modern thinking tends to dictate that the chairman is the front person for making things happen. Indeed, using Carver's definition of the board governance process—how the board itself operates—the chairman is often responsible not only to act as the primary communication link with the chief staff officer but to spearhead the activities of the board itself.

The chairman, therefore, has to use a velvet glove in demonstrating board discipline while at the same time setting the sense of direction for the board. Some would argue that a good board does not depend on a good chairman—that the function has little short-term impact. This is analogous to stating that a good orchestra can do without a good conductor. Maybe sometimes it can, but a good conductor has the ability to draw something extra out of the players. A chairman should do more than just maintain order. Chairmen should specifically not be selected on the basis of seniority or availability, but on the basis of having the potential not only to apply positive leadership—a prerequisite—but to devise their own priorities for the organization, compatible with its strategic objectives.

In the volunteer context, board chairmen are restricted in terms of authority. They can only apply or interpret the specific authority delegated by the board. While chairmen are the most senior representative of the board, they can make decisions about board processes only as long as they operate strictly within the defined terms of reference and boundaries. They have less latitude than for-profit board chairmen. This fact can work against the overall effectiveness of the not-for-profit board.

Additionally, chairmen must cope with the relationship with the chief staff officer. More than ever, the temptation to become involved in detail or trespass onto the functions specifically delegated to staff must be resisted. Micromanagement is to some extent the scourge of volunteer organizations. One reason is that in many instances, the board members must function in the oversight and strategic modes while at the same time being prepared to operate as volunteers in assisting staff. Nevertheless, in acting in the latter capacity, they become part of the chief staff officer's team and no longer wear their board hats.

BOARD/STAFF RELATIONSHIPS

Quoting Carver again in *Boards That Make a Difference*:

> From the board's point of view, the important lesson is that the board's relationship with the chief staff officer must be formed around the *accountability* of the position, not its *responsibility*. In other words, it need be none of the board's concern just what job responsibilities fall to the CSO. The board's concern is confined to what it holds the CSO accountable for.[6]

The precise language of the above quotation is important. The emphasis is on the board defining precisely *what* it holds the chief staff officer accountable for and not on the minutiae of precisely what the job involves. In a well-run organization, the precise details should be left largely, subject to monitoring and reporting, to the chief staff officer.

Volunteer boards often find it difficult to comprehend that, as in for-profit companies, all formal communications must be directed through the CSO. The CSO is basically the only staff member directly employed by the board. In theory, although courtesy and convention dictate that the board is kept completely informed (particularly regarding senior appointments), all other staff members are appointed by the CSO. The terms of reference for the chief staff officer ("executive limitations," in Carver's language) should set the boundaries within he should be allowed the flexibility to operate. This is another challenge for many volunteer boards—they like to feel they are involved in many management decisions. In the end, it is the performance of the CSO that is critical, and this can be judged fairly only if the CSO is given the scope to make operational judgments and implement the strategic decisions of the board in relatively an unfettered manner.

To counter any risk that the board feel left out, it is equally important that controls in place force the production of reports on a timely basis. The generation of this information, which is subject to the same kind of checks and balances imposed on the CEO of a for-profit enterprise, also forms part of the chief staff officer's job specifications.

The board, while keeping prudent oversight on staff activities, may tend to limit the extent of the power delegated to the CSO but not to the extent that it hampers execution. Such limitations tend to extend only to the degree of authority delegated, not to the delegation of authority itself. Control is seen as the board's involvement in the accountability process. In all other aspects, the board should be seen as being strongly supportive.

A final comment: The chief staff officer must be seen as reporting to the board as a whole, not to individual board members or the chairman. While the board may delegate, even assume, that the chairman provides the primary contact with the CSO, the chairman has no power to issue instructions that are outside the envelope of authority of the CSO, or to change or terminate the terms of his appointment without express board approval. The chairman may not like this constraint. Indeed, it is often ignored, but this not sound governance. A volunteer board operates very much in consensus mode, and the principle of collective responsibility applies in a very powerful manner.

In a volunteer organization, it is entirely possible to have two effective leaders: the chairman as leader of the board, taking initiatives in a strategic and oversight sense, and the CSO who provides internal leadership in implementing and achieving the organization's overall objectives.

LEGAL LIABILITY EXPOSURE

As this book is not a legal text, the comments here will be brief. Chapter 6 describes legal liability exposure in the context of the for-profit company. In general terms, the same principles apply in the not-for-profit sector as well.

The duties of honesty, loyalty, care, diligence, skill, and prudence all still apply. Maybe not quite so powerfully or with the degree of legal sanction, but directors of not-for-profit boards still are charged with behaving appropriately in terms of fiduciary responsibilities, conflict of interest, and so on. This is especially true if the not-for-profit organization is incorporated under one of the Corporations Acts, which, while offering an element of individual director protection, also impose statutory responsibilities.

Again, while it has occurred comparatively rarely, directors (or trustees) of not-for-profit enterprises have been found liable by the courts for misdeeds, and such liabilities can cause personal obligations and distress. Indeed, recent legislation has imposed quite onerous responsibilities on directors of not-for-profit organizations in the area involving the handling of funds and investments.

Not-for-profit boards must exercise diligence with respect to financial matters, and government taxes should be withheld and remitted. Labor, health, and environmental regulations also apply quite rigidly, particularly in relation to staff. Some volunteer organizations, including boards of directors, have been found liable for accidents and third-party incidents; this dictates a pragmatic view on insurance coverage, the availability of which parallels the for-profit sector, but usually at lower cost.

In general terms, volunteer boards have legal liability exposure comparable to that of the for-profit sector, and their behavior should be considered of similar importance.

CHAPTER 13

The Ultimate Sanction

*If you can keep your head when all about you are losing theirs
and blaming it on you.
If you can trust yourself when all men doubt you, but make
allowance for their doubting too.*

—Rudyard Kipling (1865–1936), *If*

BOARD CULTURE

Much has been made of the phrase "board culture." It tends to describe the collegiality or chemistry that is built up by a group of often disparate individuals who form the board of directors. Much of what constitutes board culture is never written down but relates to how directors interact with each other: how they behave, both in formal meetings and informally.

Sometimes the concept of board culture may be overdone, to the extent that these unwritten rules tend to entrench tradition rather than encourage innovation. Remember the autocratic chairman who insisted on all contributions being channeled through the chair, rather than allowing for direct dialogue between directors. This is an extreme example, but it happened.

New board members tend to learn conventions by listening, which is natural for someone recently elected. However, sometimes

179

there is a fine line between achieving the appropriate degree of collegiality in decision making without frustrating constructive dialogue. Clearly, a board member must fit in with colleagues but definitely not be subservient to them, even if a relative neophyte to the organization. Every director has to be prepared to stand up and be counted. By the same token, a director must come well prepared and direct her energies toward achieving consensus rather than present a radical position for which there is little support.

However, Jim Gillies, author of *Boardroom Renaissance*, tells the story where he was virtually the lone board dissenter in the takeover of Connaught Laboratories by Merieux, a French company. Gillies felt that the offer price was below what the stock was worth, even though the majority of his board colleagues were prepared to accept. After several weeks, Merieux finally increased its offer and Gillies was vindicated, but he felt isolated in his minority stand while negotiations were being conducted. Again, this is an extreme example, but it can indicate that there may be instances when a minority viewpoint, even dissension, deserves consideration.

The key to board culture is board effectiveness. A cohesive team allows for productive dialogue while also allowing the opportunity for constructive dissent. Leighton and Thain in *Making Boards Work* include a table that illustrates old and new board cultures. Reproduced in Exhibit 13.1, it highlights a number of different aspects of board operation and how old and new behavior codes apply. Their introduction to the table stated:

> We have postulated that board cultures can be broadly categorized as one of two types, the 'old' representing the more traditional and passive board, and the 'new'—professional, vigorous, challenging, dynamic and involved. In cases where the old culture prevails, it often controls the directors. In the new culture, it is the other way around. . . .[1]

Chairmen must allow a culture to develop, preferably along the new lines postulated in the exhibit. Collegiality must be encouraged while at the same time making allowances for contrary viewpoints. Above all, the chairman must inspire constructive dialogue by every member of the board, not just a few. There is little merit in a new director remaining silent on the basis that "fools rush in where angels fear to tread." True, board members must be allowed time to find their feet, but there is no probationary period. If talent has been chosen carefully, the opportunity to participate in a meaningful manner can come relatively quickly.

Exhibit 13.1 The Old and New Board Cultures.

BEHAVIOR CODE		
	Old	**New**
Approach	Passive	Active
Function	Ratification	Leadership
Style	Reactive	Assertive
CULTURE		
Beliefs	Directors are honoured guests, cheerleader, to support management	Directors are trustees, consultant, leadership agent, for shareholders
Values	Prestige, ego, selfish, exclusiveness, shrewd politics, autocracy	Servant leadership, professionalism, management excellence, democracy, collegiality
Attitudes	Follow the group, be compatible	Be responsible, take charge, dissent as appropriate
Norms	Guardedness, political correctness	Openness, problem oriented
Traditions	Formality, indirectness	Informality, directness
Rituals	Process, politics	Penetrating analysis, group discussion
Heroes	Powerful, wealthy, tough CEOs	Professional, modern leadership managers, innovators, Alfred Sloan types
Role Models	Old fashioned, macho CEOs	Counsellors and coaches, turnaround specialists

Source: David S. R. Leighton and Donald H. Thain, *Making Boards Work: What Directors Must Do to Make Canadian Boards Effective* (McGraw-Hill Ryerson Ltd., 1997), p. 227. Used with permission.

ANTICIPATING BOARDROOM PROBLEMS

Thus far the text has focused on the chairman of the board as independent of management. In other words, a different person is the chief executive officer. In many instances, however, this is not the case. In Canada joint tenure is probably around the 30 percent mark, while in the United States it is probably quite a bit higher. The problem with joint tenure is that the actual jobs of chairman and CEO are significantly different. Also, the required personality and character traits can be quite different as well. Hence it follows that not all CEOs can make a successful transition to chairman or are they successful in combining the positions. Appointing a senior independent member of the board as lead director to balance such a concentration of power is merely a stopgap cure. It tends to allow the perpetuation of a practice that most analysts feel is outmoded.

Problems can arise, therefore, when a strong CEO who is also chairman or a previous CEO who has now become chairman does not appreciate fully the need to achieve consensus by managing *by* committee rather than *in* committee. Such people often believe in presenting a strong driving personality; being a driver rather than a leader. In the extreme, such people can veer heavily toward autocracy.

While such behavior could have a place in a turnaround situation or in conditions of adversity where little flexibility in decision-making exists, boards generally find it difficult to react or perform at their best in such situations. The collegiality process can turn to brittleness or a rubber-stamping mentality; both attitudes constrain effective dialogue and exchanges of views. Alternatively, ideas and suggestions may be suppressed because of the overpowering influence of the chair. Obviously serious governance dangers are present when these circumstances exist.

What is a board to do under these conditions? The most likely course of action would be for one or two of the most senior independent directors to take the chairman to task in a private discussion. They should make it quite clear that the board's team spirit is being jeopardized, which is counterproductive both to the individuals concerned and to the company as a whole. If it continues without serious change, then potential and undermining board resignations will likely follow.

At the other extreme, sometimes chairmen do not have strong personalities and are intimidated by the pressures of the role or, indeed, by the personalities of some of the independent directors (who may have been appointed by, and are therefore nominees of, a major shareholder). The potential conflict here is to maintain an equitable balance of interests while stimulating satisfactory board performance.

What is the effect of major shareholders having the right to nominate directors to a board? In many instances this could tend to undermine minority shareholder interests. In Canada in particular, and increasingly in the United States, concentration of ownership is such that conglomerate owners and institutional investors exercise control, either individually or in concert, over a substantial majority of major publicly listed companies, either directly or indirectly. How such investors use their muscle in governance terms is problematical. Rarely are minority shareholder interests considered separately, as it is assumed that what is best for the majority must be equally good for the minority.

Sometimes boards disregard the legal requirements for all shareholders' interests to be considered equally. However, we also recognize sometimes it may be difficult for board chairmen to handle situations where major shareholder interests are being pressed by their board nominees. Situations like this can challenge the whole system of governance. To date, legislative and regulatory powers have not been widely used in remedying any but the most blatant transgressions.

Clearly, the free enterprise system must flourish with the minimum of government involvement. But at the same time, it must demonstrate responsible self-regulation. Until comparatively recently, some of the worst offenders were some financial institutions themselves, in particular mutual funds. Their view of effective corporate governance practices appeared to be significantly different from the intent of the various published corporate governance guidelines.

The massive pension funds CALpers and TIAA-CREF in the United States have set excellent examples by which they attempt proactively to influence the governance of investee companies, particularly the poor performers. Comparable institutions in Canada have so far been reluctant to exercise their muscle other than by the use of their proxy voting power, a policy that may or may not be effective. Early in 2001, one or two of the largest Canadian pension funds began to publicize their use of proxy voting influence to disagree with a company's voting recommendations.

How should chairmen deal with dissident and nonperforming directors? The latter are probably the easier of the challenges. The nominating committee must be charged with finding appropriate replacements. In the case of a nominee, a frank and direct approach to the nominating shareholder is often the most effective way to remove a poor performer. If it is a high-profile individual who has taken on too many directorship roles to allow adequate involvement, again a direct but diplomatic approach is often all that is necessary.

Dissident directors are more difficult to handle. Dissent must be carefully analyzed to determine its cause. Sometimes constructive dissent is both helpful and necessary. Sometimes a board gets too close to the forest and does not see the trees, in which case a director drawing attention to the situation can deserve an accolade—definitely not criticism. Unfortunately, not everyone has the gift of dissenting tactfully. Some directors, even if in the right, are so irritating that their colleagues refuse to listen to reason.

In such circumstances, probably a good course of action would be for the chairman to adjourn the meeting to allow passions to cool. Sometimes tabling the contentious matter to a future meeting provides the opportunity for wise heads to prevail in private rather than allow open confrontation. Only if repeated dissension occurs should the chairman talk, one on one, with the dissenting parties to see if an approach can be agreed to that allows board chemistry to be reestablished.

While dissension is not necessarily a bad thing, it must be controlled. Differences of opinion, in general, should not be allowed to become confrontations. Confrontations are no-win situations. Personal reputations suddenly become important, resulting in the risk of loss of face, and compromise becomes much more difficult. Whatever happens, if major contention occurs, the chairman has an obligation to close the discussion at the earliest opportunity. Sometimes chairmen are criticized for trying to do this, accused of not allowing free debate. Nevertheless, the chairman must explain that further discussion at this point could be counterproductive and emphasize that the subject of discussion is not dead, merely postponed to allow a little breathing space. In such situations, the chairman must make every attempt to contain the debate to the boardroom, even to the extent of asking nonboard members to leave immediately should things begin to get lively, and ensuring that the minutes reflect decisions, not acrimonious debate.

What about the problem of dealing with management performance, or lack of it? Here a critical scenario, not one that can be adjusted using performance appraisal techniques, is the focus. If the chairman is also CEO, tackling this task could be difficult. In most such situations, precipitous action is taken much later than it should have been. Boards traditionally are reluctant to criticize the CEO, unless things are so blatantly wrong that it becomes inevitable. Many of the high-profile CEO dismissals of the 1990s fell into this category.

Performance evaluation procedures have their place in steady-state situations or where remuneration is being discussed. But in a crisis scenario, sometimes the situation has come quite suddenly to the board's attention. Either there has been deliberate deception or something not anticipated that should have been has come to a head, such as predictions of a major financial shortfall. Here some positive action is paramount for the sake of public relations and image, stability of share price, satisfying investors and shareholders, and a host of other good reasons. A recent example of this occurring is the replacement of the CEO of Ford Motor Company in the United States.

The board should consider strongly going into closed session without employee directors, even the CEO (even if he is also chairman) present. Board members should attempt to work through whatever is necessary, seeking outside professional advice whenever appropriate. On these types of occasions, board members must be prepared to stand up and be counted and make whatever kind of tough decision is required. The chairman or the lead independent director must demonstrate positive leadership. Deferring a decision is not likely to ameliorate the predicament in this situation.

Incidentally, this is a very similar scenario to when a key figure suddenly becomes disabled or dies. The company must continue as best it can, and the chairman must orchestrate things with as little disruption as possible. The motto is "short-term pain for long-term gain."

DANGER SIGNALS

Much has been made of the danger of rubber-stamping and endorsing the actions of others by default. Doing this includes the acceptance of committee reports and actions implicit within them, including actions of a committee mandated to meet more frequently than the main board, and the assumption of some board responsibilities by such a committee.

If the board is content with acts that tend to bypass the scrutiny of the full board, and the chairman has a positive role to play in examining each occurrence in detail, then expediency can dictate more of a routine acceptance. However, the board must, in all circumstances, take definite and positive action to approve all decisions.

Whatever the scenario, the board must insist on:

- Full and accurate information
- Being given sufficient time to seek amplification and explanation
- Not being pressured either unreasonably nor unduly
- Being prepared to approve conditionally but not necessarily unequivocally

Robert Kirk Mueller wrote in *New Directions for Directors*:

Directors have a clear responsibility to engage in freedom of thought and speech. Interference in such is both illegal and immoral. This obligation is considered much more seriously in the governance of academic institutions. However, this responsibility does apply [also] to economic institutions. There is a clear responsibility for corporate directors to make sure there are opportunities to ventilate differences in perspective, opinions and disagreements, and perhaps even engage in an occasional fervid confrontation. The problem with most boards of directors is not that they are too disputatious, but that they are not disputatious enough—if at all in many cases. Directors should have a sharp conscience about the privation and protection of expressions of opinion, no matter whom they may offend.[2]

Therefore, the board must be neither captive to management nor operate without regard for it. The board must provide for checks and balances and discuss matters in an informed manner and with an independent perspective. At the same time, the board must be satisfied that it is exercising due diligence. Directors may disagree when they feel:

- They are being improperly or insufficiently briefed
- The company is embarking on improper or incorrect procedures
- The company is indulging in actions that may be unethical, even illegal

The chairman has an obligation to ensure that the agenda for board meetings is designed to disclose every eventuality that should be brought before the board, whether for decision or informational purposes. In order for this to occur, the chairman must be closely involved with the CEO and other senior officers, such as the heads of the financial and operational activities. A danger signal is when CEOs feel that everything should be channeled through them.

Companies get into trouble because they have either made the wrong decision (or a partial decision where a more energetic action was required), or they have neglected to take a necessary course of action. Misjudging or mistiming decisions regarding threats and opportunities are key examples.

Failure to recognize income appropriately is another instance where companies can quickly get into trouble, by taking into income business that is not assured, by overtrading, or by manipulating inventory or work in progress. All are quagmires that are difficult to detect unless internal audit procedures are both in place and operating satisfactorily.

Boards should operate on the principle of no surprises. Corrective action may be obvious with the use of hindsight, but a savvy board always will discuss any potential threat to profitability and continued viability and have in place at least a semblance of a contingency plan should things go wrong. Every company assumes risk in its day-to-day activities. Correct business judgment is not always sacrosanct. The chairman must take a pragmatic role in assessing the effects of risk and act as a foil to the CEO's enthusiasm where necessary.

HANDLING DISAGREEMENT AND DISSENT

A chairman must be very sensitive to signs of dissent or disagreement among colleagues. A discerning chairman can sense when attitudes are becoming tense and meetings turn more into the thrust and parry of a confrontation rather than a means of conducting dialogue so as to reach consensus. Reading these signs and interpreting them correctly requires shrewdness and insight.

Conversely, chairmen must not act negatively when their own judgment and performance is questioned. They are also human beings and therefore not infallible. How else is a chairman to realize shortcomings if not subjected to the occasional question or challenge? Chapter 1 listed the leadership qualities mandatory for a good chairman. Sometimes these skills need to be sharpened or renewed.

So far the text has considered that most board members and board chairmen are competent and fit for their roles. What happens if they are not? The board is there to direct the enterprise so as to increase shareholder value, remain viable, and make a profit. These are its primary roles. The key to their achievement is effective decision making and oversight of management in implementing such decisions.

If directors turn out to lack the intrinsic ability or the interpersonal skills (or fail to attend meetings regularly), then they should be persuaded to resign by the chairman and/or the chairman of the nominating committee. If the selection process is flawed, or if insufficient effort is spent in orientating and training new directors, then the board must improve such procedures in short order. Above all, the performance evaluation procedures set out in Chapter 8 must be considered as a key developmental tool.

The chairman must never fail to manage the board process—*how* it operates. To do so, directors must know what is expected of them. A job specification is an essential tool. Directors must learn not to speak from the seat of their pants or to be instant decision makers. They must do their homework, and the chairman should attempt, with sensitivity and diplomacy, to ensure that they do.

The chairman should be aware of the dangers of group factions. Boards should never be allowed to develop into disparate elements that regularly are pitched against each other. Such a situation could occur when there are significant nominees appointed by major shareholders or appointed by a parent company to a subsidiary board. In such instances, the chairman should make every effort to have the independence and autonomy of the board clearly defined, in writing, so that everyone clearly understands the envelope within which it operates.

Directors who believe that they represent other constituencies rather than all shareholders equally should be disabused of this notion. This may be a very difficult task. Majority shareholder directors have been known to march in and dictate terms to the board completely contrary to every facet of sound, even legal, corporate governance. However, if they have the backing of controlling shareholder power, there is little a chairman can do other than try to persuade them of the consequences of their actions or, in the ultimate, tender his resignation.

Chairmen should never allow themselves to become captive to the will of others if this compromises the definition of director independence. Chairmen have an all-important role in managing disagreement and dissent. How they do so is largely how they use personality and powers of persuasion. Diffusing a situation by allowing dissenters to run out of steam is one way that is often successful. In the long run, while occasional dissent and disagreement may be considered a healthy phenomenon, the chairman should work to avoid it as far as possible. While this may seem contradictory, a climate of consensus and collegiality is always preferable to confrontation (assuming that the board is proactive and challenges assumptions to the extent that management and others around the board table are kept on their toes).

The chairman's job, indeed any board position, will never be a sinecure or an accolade. It is, and always will be, extremely hard work, but the results can be remarkably gratifying.

NOTES

Introduction

1. Sir Adrian Cadbury, *The Company Chairman* (Director Books, 1990), p. 2.
2. Ibid., p. 10.

Chapter 1

1. Hugh Parker, *Letters to a New Chairman* (Director Publications, 1979), p. 7.
2. Robert Kirk Mueller, *New Directions for Directors: Behind the Bylaws* (Lexington Books, D.C. Heath and Company, 1978), p. 90.
3. Sir Adrian Cadbury, *The Company Chairman* (Director Books, 1990), p. 93.

Chapter 2

1. William Houston and Nigel Lewis, *The Independent Director: Handbook and Guide to Corporate Governance* (Butterworth–Heinemann, 1992), p. 6.
2. Kenneth Lindon-Travers, *Non-Executive Directors: A Guide to Their Responsibilities & Appointment* (Director Books, 1990), p. 159.
3. J. M. Wainberg, *Duties and Responsibilities of Directors in Canada* (CCH Canadian, 1987).
4. Lindon-Travers, *Non-Executive Directors,* p. 153.
5. Brian P. Smith, *The Non-Executive Director* (PA Management Consultants Limited, ca. 1971), p. 4.
6. Edward P. Mattar and Michael Ball, eds., *Handbook for Corporate Directors* (McGraw-Hill Book Company, 1985), p. 24.3.
7. Sir Kenneth Cork, *The Code of Practice for the Non-Executive Director* (Institute of Directors).
8. Lindon-Travers, *Non-Executive Directors,* p. 172.
9. *Boardroom* newsletter (January/February 2001), p. 4.
10. Sir Graham Day, *Boardroom* newsletter (March 1996), p. 2.
11. Bill Dimma, "Best Practices: Some Personal Experiences as a Director," *Professional Administrator* (Winter 2000), p. 14. Used with permission.
12. Editorial, *Boardroom* newsletter (January/February 2001), p. 1.

13. *The Independent Corporate Director: Recommendations and Guidance on Boardroom Practice* (Institute of Corporate Directors, 1988).

Chapter 3

1. James Gillies, *Boardroom Renaissance: Power, Morality and Performance in the Modern Corporation* (McGraw-Hill Ryerson, 1992), p. 67. Used with permission.
2. J. W. Lorsch and E. MacIver, *Pawns or Potentates: The Reality of America's Corporate Boards* (Harvard Business School Press, 1989).
3. James Gillies, *Boardroom Renaissance*, p. 67.
4. *Boardroom* newsletter (September/October 2001), p. 1.
5. Robert Kirk Mueller, *New Directions for Directors: Behind the Bylaws* (Lexington Books, D.C. Heath and Company, 1978), p. 69.
6. Cadbury Committee Report, *The Financial Aspects of Corporate Governance*, extract from the *Code of Best Practice* (London Stock Exchange, 1992).
7. *Combined Code for Corporate Governance* (London Stock Exchange, 1999).
8. Report of the Toronto Stock Exchange Committee on Corporate Governance in Canada, *Where Were the Directors? Guidelines for Improved Corporate Governance in Canada* (Toronto Stock Exchange, December 1994), p. 5.
9. *Boardroom* newsletter (January/February 2000), p. 1.
10. Sir Adrian Cadbury, *The Company Chairman* (Director Books, 1990), p. 16.
11. David S. R. Leighton and Donald H. Thain, *Making Boards Work: What Directors Must Do to Make Canadian Boards Effective* (McGraw-Hill Ryerson Ltd, 1997), p. 146. Used with permission.
12. Kevin Brown, "Playing by the Rules," UK *Director* magazine (January 2000). Used with permission.
13. Thomas Kierans, from an address made to the Institute for International Research Corporate Governance Congress, Toronto, October 6, 1996, reported in *Boardroom* newsletter (January 1997).
14. Ibid.

Chapter 4

1. *Guidelines for Directors* (Institute of Directors, 1985), p. 18.
2. William Houston and Nigel Lewis, *The Independent Director: Handbook and Guide to Corporate Governance* (Butterworth–Heinemann, 1992), p. 8.
3. Edward P. Mattar and Michael Ball, eds., *Handbook for Corporate Directors* (McGraw-Hill Book Company, 1985), p. 7.1.

Chapter 5

1. Kenichi Ohmae, *The Mind of the Strategist: The Art of Japanese Business* (McGraw-Hill Book Company, 1982).

2. Bob Garratt, ed., *Developing Strategic Thought* (HarperCollins Publishers, 1995), p. 29.

3. David Hargreaves, "Do's and Don'ts in Corporate Planning," UK *Financial Times*, September 26, 1967. Used with permission.

Chapter 6

1. *Duties and Responsibilities of Directors in Canada* (CCH Canadian, 1987).

2. UK *Financial Director* (VNU Business Publications, July/August 1996). Used with permission.

3. Ibid. Used with permission.

4. Ibid. Used with permission.

5. Ken McPherson, Report of the South Australia Auditor General (South Australia Government Publication, 1991), vol. 1, pp. 1.5–3.6.

6. Charles A. Anderson and Robert N. Anthony, *The New Corporate Directors: Insights for Board Members & Executives* (John Wiley & Sons, 1986), p. 26.

7. Report of the Toronto Stock Exchange Committee on Corporate Disclosure (The Allen Report), *Responsible Corporate Disclosure: A Search for Balance* (Toronto Stock Exchange, 1997), p. ix.

8. Margot Priest, R. Mecredy-Williams, Barbara R. C. Doherty, James W. O'Reilly, *Directors' Duties in Canada: Managing Risk* (CCH Canadian Limited, 1995), p. 115.

9. Final Report of the Royal Commission into the Tricontinental Group of Companies (Australian Government Publication, 1992).

10. *AWA Limited v. Daniels* (The Supreme Court of New South Wales Court of Appeal Judgment, May 1995), p. 256.

11. Henry Bosch, *The Director at Risk*, p. 110.

12. Final Report of the Royal Commission into the Tricontinental Group of Companies, August 1992.

13. Sir Ronnie Hampel, chair, *Report on Corporate Governance* (London Stock Exchange, 1999).

14. Institute of Chartered Accountants of England and Wales, the Turnbull Report, *Internal Control: Guidance for Directors on the Combined Code* (Institute of Chartered Accountants of England and Wales, 1999).

15. Patrick J. Caragata, *Business Early Warning Systems: Corporate Governance for the New Millennium* (Butterworths [New Zealand], 1999), p. 125. Used with permission.

16. Kevin Brown, "Playing by the Rules," *Director* magazine (UK Institute of Directors, January 2000). Used with permission.

Chapter 7

1. Ralph D. Ward, *21st Century Corporate Board* (John Wiley & Sons, 1997), p. 204.

2. David S. R. Leighton and Donald H. Thain, *Making Boards Work: What Directors Must Do to Make Canadian Boards Effective* (McGraw-Hill Ryerson Ltd, 1997), p. 286. Used with permission.

3. Report of the NACD Blue Ribbon Commission, *Audit Committees: A Practical Guide* (National Association of Corporate Directors and the Center for Board Leadership, 1999), p. vii.

4. Ibid., p. 34.

5. Interim Report of the Joint Committee on Corporate Governance (the Saucier Committee), *Beyond Compliance: Building a Governance Culture* (Institute of Chartered Accountants of Canada, TSE and CDNX, March 2001).

6. J. E. Richard, *Compensation Committee Manual,* 4th ed. (J. Richard & Co., 1999), p. I–1.

7. *Corporate Director's Guidebook,* 2nd ed. (American Bar Association, 1997).

8. Editorial, UK *Director* magazine (October 1994).

9. Report of the Toronto Stock Exchange Committee on Corporate Governance in Canada, *Where Were the Directors? Guidelines for Improved Corporate Governance in Canada* (Toronto Stock Exchange, December 1994), p. 4.

10. James Gillies, *Boardroom Renaissance: Power, Morality and Performance in the Modern Corporation* (McGraw-Hill Ryerson, 1992), p. 69. Used with permission.

11. Bryan Burrough and John Helyar, *Barbarians at the Gate: The Fall of RJR Nabisco* (HarperTrade, 1990).

12. James Gillies, *Boardroom Renaissance,* p. 62. Used with permission.

13. Kevin Brown, "Playing by the Rules," UK *Director* magazine (January 2000). Used with permission.

14. Leighton and Thain, *Making Boards Work,* p. 250. Used with permission.

Chapter 8

1. Robert Mueller, *New Directions for Directors: Behind the Bylaws* (Lexington Books, D.C. Heath and Company, 1978).

2. Robert Mueller, *Directors & Boards: A Director's Performance Appraisal* (Investment Dealers' Digest, Spring 1993).

3. Report of the Toronto Stock Exchange Committee on Corporate Governance in Canada, *Where Were the Directors? Guidelines for Improved Corporate Governance in Canada* (Toronto Stock Exchange, December 1994), p. 5.

4. Ibid., p. 28.

5. Robert Kirk Mueller, *New Directions for Directors: Behind the Bylaws* (Lexington Books, D.C. Heath and Company, 1978), p. 54.

Chapter 9

1. Sir Ronnie Hampel, chair, *Report on Corporate Governance* (London Stock Exchange, 1999).

2. Henry Mintzberg, *The Rise and Fall of Strategic Planning* (Free Press and Prentice Hall International, 1994).

3. Patrick J. Caragata, *Business Early Warning Systems: Corporate Governance for the New Millennium* (Butterworths [New Zealand], 1999), p. 181. Used with permission.

4. Stuart, Rock, ed., *Getting the Family to Work Together; Pay, Benefits and Incentives in Family Companies; Succession Management in Family Companies; The Role of "Outsiders" in Family Companies.* Family Business Management Series. UK Institute of Directors and the Stoy Centre for Family Business (Director Publications, 1995–1997).

5. Howard M. Schilit, *What Directors Can Do to Prevent and Detect Financial Shenanigans: Red Flags and Action Steps for Directors Concerned About Fraud* (National Association of Corporate Directors, 1994). Used with permission.

6. Tom Kierans, in "Maximising Board Effectiveness," *Boardroom* newsletter (January 1997), p. 5.

7. Robert K. Mueller, *The Director's and Officer's Guide to Advisory Boards* (Quorum Books, 1990), p. 43.

8. "Motorola: Training for the Millennium," *Business Week* magazine, March 28, 1994.

9. Mueller, *The Director's and Officer's Guide to Advisory Boards*, p. 142.

10. Extract from an address by David A. H. Brown at the 2001 Conference Board of Canada Corporate Governance Conference entitled "Springboard to Excellence."

Chapter 10

1. Marie Jennings, *The Guide to Good Corporate Citizenship* (Director Books, 1990), p. vii.

2. "Cybercrime," *Financial Times* (London), July 16, 2000.

3. Rio Tinto plc, "The Way We Work: Our Statement of Business Practice," *Boardroom* (July 1998), p. 1.

4. Extract from an address by Lord Holme of Cheltenham to the Commonwealth Conference on Corporate Governance held in the United Kingdom, May 1998.

5. Rio Tinto plc, "The Way We Work: Our Statement of Business Practice," *Boardroom* (July 1998), p. 3.

Chapter 11

1. New Zealand Institute of Directors, *Boardroom* newsletter (October 1994).

2. James Gillies, *Boardroom Renaissance: Power, Morality and Performance in the Modern Corporation* (McGraw-Hill Ryerson, 1992), p. 211. Used with permission.

3. Extract from a presentation made by Yves Michaud to the Corporate Directors' Summit, presented by Insight Information Services, October 1997; reported in *Boardroom* newsletter (November 1997).
4. Extract from a presentation made by Terence Corcoran to the Corporate Secretaries' Congress, organized by the Institute for International Research, September 1998; reported in *Boardroom* newsletter (November 1998).
5. Patrick J. Caragata, *Business Early Warning Systems: Corporate Governance for the New Millennium* (Butterworths [New Zealand], 1999).
6. Sir Adrian Cadbury, *The Company Chairman* (Director Books, 1990), p. 154.

Chapter 12

1. Broadbent Report, *Building on Strength: Improving Governance and Accountability in Canada's Voluntary Sector* (Panel on Accountability and Governance in the Voluntary Sector, 1999), p. 13.
2. Ibid., p. 11.
3. Smith, Bucklin & Associates, *The Complete Guide to Nonprofit Management* (John Wiley & Sons, 1994), p. 41.
4. John Carver, *Boards That Make a Difference: A New Design for Leadership in Nonprofit and Public Organizations* (Jossey-Bass, 1990), p. 19.
5. John Carver, executive editor, *Board Leadership: Policy Governance in Action* (newsletter), (Jossey-Bass, 2000).
6. Carver, *Boards That Make a Difference*, p. 114.

Chapter 13

1. David S. R. Leighton and Donald H. Thain, *Making Boards Work: What Directors Must Do to Make Canadian Boards Effective* (McGraw-Hill Ryerson, 1997), pp. 226–227. Used with permission.
2. Robert Kirk Mueller, *New Directions for Directors: Behind the Bylaws* (Lexington Books, D.C. Heath and Company, 1978), p. 68.

BIBLIOGRAPHY

Allen Report, Report of the Toronto Stock Exchange Committee on Corporate Disclosure. *Responsible Corporate Disclosure.* Toronto Stock Exchange Committee on Corporate Disclosure, 1997.

Anderson, Charles A., and Robert N. Anthony. *The New Corporate Directors: Insights for Board Members and Executives.* John Wiley & Sons, 1986.

Australian Institute of Company Directors. *Code of Conduct.* 1996.

Bosch, Henry. *The Director at Risk: Accountability in the Boardroom.* FT Pitman Publishing/Pearson Professional (Australia) Pty Ltd., 1995.

Braiotta, Louis, and A. A. Sommer, Jr. *The Essential Guide to Effective Corporate Board Committees.* Prentice-Hall, 1987.

Brown, David A. H., and Debra L. Brown. *Planning to Prevail: A Practical Guide to the Board's Role in Strategic Planning and Performance Measurement.* Conference Board of Canada, May 2000.

CACG Guidelines: Principles for Corporate Governance in the Commonwealth. Commonwealth Association for Corporate Governance, November 1999.

Cadbury, Sir Adrian. *The Company Chairman.* Director Books, 1990.

Caragata, Patrick J. *Business Early Warning Systems: Corporate Governance for the New Millennium.* Butterworths (New Zealand), 1999.

Carver, John. *Boards That Make a Difference: A New Design for Leadership in Nonprofit and Public Organizations.* Jossey-Bass, 1990.

Conger, Jay, Edward Lawler III, and David Finegold. *Corporate Boards: New Strategies for Adding Value at the Top.* Jossey-Bass, 2001.

Corbin, Ruth M. *Report on Corporate Governance 1999: Five Years to the Dey.* Toronto Stock Exchange, 1999.

Corporate Director's Guidebook, 2nd ed. American Bar Association, 1997.

Danco, Leon A., and Donald J. Jonovic. *Outside Directors in the Family Owned Business.* Center for Family Business, 1987.

Dauphinais, G. William, Grady Means, and Colin Price, eds. *Wisdom of the CEO.* John Wiley & Sons, 2000.

Dimma, William. *Excellence in the Boardroom: Best Practices in Corporate Directorship.* John Wiley & Sons Canada, 2002.

Dunne, Patrick. *Running Board Meetings.* Kogan Page, 1997.

Francis, Ivor. *Future Direction: The Power of the Competitive Board.* FT Pitman Publishing/Pearson Professional (Australia) Pty Ltd., 1997.

Garratt, Bob. *The Fish Rots from the Head.* HarperCollins, 1996.

Garratt, Bob, ed. *Developing Strategic Thought.* HarperCollins, 1995.

Gillies, James. *Boardroom Renaissance: Power, Morality and Performance in the Modern Corporation.* McGraw-Hill Ryerson, 1992.

Harper, John. *Chairing the Board: A Practical Guide to Activities and Responsibilities.* Kogan Page, 2000.

Hilmer, Frederick G. *Strictly Boardroom: Improving Governance to Enhance Company Performance.* Business Library/Information Australia, 1993.

Houston, William, and Nigel Lewis. *The Independent Director: Handbook and Guide to Corporate Governance.* Butterworth–Heinemann, 1992.

Institute of Corporate Directors. *Guidelines for Corporate Directors.* 1987, rev. 1992.

Institute of Corporate Directors. *The Independent Corporate Director: Recommendations and Guidance on Boardroom Practice.* 1988.

Institute of Directors. *The Company Director's Guide: Your Duties, Responsibilities & Liabilities.* Kogan Page, 2001.

Institute of Directors. *Good Practice for Directors: Standards for the Board.* Author, 1995.

Jennings, Marie. *The Guide to Good Corporate Citizenship.* Director Books, 1990.

Leighton, David S. R., and Donald H. Thain. *Making Boards Work: What Directors Must Do to Make Canadian Boards Effective.* McGraw-Hill Ryerson, 1997.

Lindon-Travers, Ken. *Non-Executive Directors: A Guide to Their Responsibilities and Appointment.* Director Books, 1990.

Lorsch, J. W., and E. MacIver. *Pawns or Potentates: The Reality of America's Corporate Boards.* Harvard Business School Press, 1989.

Mattar, Edward P., and Michael Ball, eds. *Handbook for Corporate Directors.* McGraw-Hill, 1985.

McGregor, Lynn. *The Human Face of Corporate Governance.* Palgrave, 2000.

Mills, Geoffrey. *On the Board,* 2nd ed. George Allen & Unwin, 1985.

Mintzberg, Henry. *The Rise and Fall of Strategic Planning.* Free Press/Prentice-Hall, 1994.

Mueller, Robert K. *The Director's and Officer's Guide to Advisory Boards.* Quorum Books, 1990.

Mueller, Robert K. *New Directions for Directors: Behind the Bylaws.* Lexington Books, D. C. Heath, 1978.

NACD Blue Ribbon Commission Report. *Audit Committees: A Practical Guide.* National Association of Corporate Directors and the Center for Board Leadership, 1999.

Ohmae, Kenichi. *The Mind of the Strategist: The Art of Japanese Business.* McGraw-Hill, 1991.

Panel on Accountability and Governance in the Voluntary Sector. *Building on Strength: Improving Governance and Accountability in Canada's Voluntary Sector.* 1999.

Parker, Hugh. *Letters to a New Chairman.* Director Publications, 1979.

Perry, Herb. *Call to Order: Meeting Rules and Procedures for Non-Profit Organizations.* Big Bay Publishing, 1989.

Phan, Phillip H. *Taking Back the Boardroom: Better Directing for the New Millennium.* McGraw-Hill (Singapore), 2000.

Pierce, Chris, ed. *The Effective Director: The Essential Guide to Director and Board Development.* Kogan Page, 2001.

PricewaterhouseCoopers. *Audit Committee Effectiveness—What Works Best.* Institute of Internal Auditors Research Foundation, 2000.

PricewaterhouseCoopers. *Corporate Governance and the Board—What Works Best.* Institute of Internal Auditors Research Foundation, 2000.

Priest, Margot, R. Mecredy-Williams, Barbara R. C. Doherty, and James W. O'Reilly. *Directors' Duties in Canada: Managing Risk.* CCH Canadian Limited, 1995.

Richard, J. E. *Compensation Committee Manual,* 4th ed. J. Richard & Co., 1999.

Rock, Stuart, ed. *Getting the Family to Work Together; Succession Management in Family Companies; The Role of "Outsiders" in Family Companies; Pay, Benefits and Incentives in Family Companies.* Family Business Management Series, UK Institute of Directors and the Stoy Centre for Family Business. Director Publications, 1995–1997.

Rock, Stuart. *Family Firms.* Director Books, 1991.

Saucier Committee/Interim Report of the Joint Committee on Corporate Governance. *Beyond Compliance: Building a Governance Culture.* March 2001; final report, November 2001.

Shultz, Susan F. *The Board Book.* American Management Association, 2001.

Smith, Bucklin, & Associates. *The Complete Guide to Nonprofit Management.* Robert H. Wilbur, Susan Kudla Finn, and Carolyn M. Freeland, eds. John Wiley & Sons, 1994.

Toronto Stock Exchange Committee on Corporate Governance in Canada. *Where Were the Directors? Guidelines for Improved Corporate Governance in Canada.* 1994.

Turnbull Report. *Internal Control: Guidance for Directors on the Combined Code.* Institute of Chartered Accountants of England and Wales, 1999.

Ward, Ralph D. *Improving Corporate Boards: The Boardroom Insider Guidebook.* John Wiley & Sons, 2000.

Ward, Ralph D. *21st Century Corporate Board.* John Wiley & Sons, 1997.

Wootton, Simon, and Terry Horne. *Strategic Thinking—A Step-by-Step Approach to Strategy.* Kogan Page, 2000.

INDEX